Denis O'Connor trained as a psychologist and teacher. Throughout his career he taught in schools and lectured in colleges and universities. He holds a Doctorate in Education and Psychology and has contributed widely to academic books and journals. *Paw Tracks in the Moonlight* is an account of an extra special period in his life. He is retired and presently lives with his wife Catherine, and three male Maine Coon cats, Pablo, Louis and Max, in a remote country cottage in Northumberland.

PAW TRACKS
IN THE
MOONLIGHT

Denis O'Connor

Illustrations by
Richard Morris

Constable · London

Constable & Robinson Ltd
3 The Lanchesters
162 Fulham Palace Road
London W6 9ER
www.constablerobinson.com

First published in the UK in 2004 by Coon Cat Books,
Ivy Cottage, West Thirston, Morpeth,
Northumberland NE65 9EF

This edition published by Constable,
an imprint of Constable & Robinson Ltd, 2009

A copy of the British Library Cataloguing in Publication Data
is available from the British Library.

978-1-84901-119-8

Printed and bound in the EU

This book is dedicated to the memory of my maternal grandmother, Elizabeth Robinson, and to my mother, Isabelle O'Connor, both of whom nurtured my love of nature and especially cats.

I also wish to acknowledge the support and encouragement of my wife Catherine, without the help of whom this book would not have been possible.

I am indebted to Richard Morris for the artistic talent he brought to the production of the illustrations in this book. Normally a landscape painter specializing in marine subjects, his insightful and vivid interpretations of the text bring the story alive.

I have spread my dreams under your feet;
Tread softly because you tread on my dreams.

W.B. Yeats, *He wishes for the cloths of heaven*

CONTENTS

WINTER: THE RESCUE

The icy January storm wailed through the crannies and spouts of the large old house as I stared at the scrubbed wooden table in the clinic of the vet, Scott Mackenzie. On the table lay a tragic sight. The silver-coloured she-cat was still bleeding, her flanks heaving with the desperate effort to stay alive. Next to her lay the barely living bodies of her two kittens. With immense difficulty I had rescued them and rushed them here for help.

'There'll be nothing I can be doing for any of them. They're all goners!' he said, with professional finality.

His Scottish brogue was oddly comforting in that sterile, clinical atmosphere. His examination had been short but thorough. I could see expressed in the eyes of Mac the Vet the professional conclusion that saving these cats was beyond the scope and skills of modern veterinary science.

'They're past hope, laddie,' he intoned gently, perhaps fearful of my reaction.

I winced at his words, not wanting to believe him as I gazed once more at the threesome lying before me on the table. Mac was right, of course, his expertise was beyond question. From appearances nothing humanely could be done for these creatures other than a swift and painless death but I had stubbornly clung on to the hope that some-how they could be saved. In my optimism I had imagined that Mac could work a miracle and restore them to health. Then I would take the whole family home with me. I lived alone and, although I had a demanding professional life, I had long toyed with the idea of having a pet, but had never got around to acquiring one. As I looked at them again, the small hope I'd nursed started to die. They did appear to be beyond help.

The she-cat was obviously too far gone to save. I imag-ined that her scrawny body had once been beautiful, with its silver-grey fur and elegant tail, but she was drifting help-lessly in and out of consciousness as she struggled to survive.

'She'll have to be put down,' Mac said in his no-nonsense manner. 'And it would be a mercy for the kittens to go as well,' he concluded. 'They're far too young to fend for them-selves even if they survive.'

He left the room with the mother, intent on doing what had to be done. While he was away, I looked down at the two kittens. Both of them were male, 'Tommies' as Mac called them. One was coloured smoky blue-grey and the other was black, with minute white markings. Neither was any bigger than a shrew. Sorrowfully, I reached down to touch them, simply as a gesture of compassion. There was no warmth nor any other sign of life in the grey kitten's body but when my fingers stroked the black-and-white kitten he stirred ever so slightly and I thought I heard a faint sigh. Suddenly, the kitten moved, curling its tiny body as if to cuddle up to the warmth of my hand. Startled, I looked down again at this little waif. It had certainly moved but I didn't know whether this was because it was in the throes of death or not.

I found myself becoming very angry. 'Cats are very special creatures. It's grossly unfair that things like this should be allowed to happen,' I said to myself, overcome by the strength of my feelings.

I recalled long-forgotten incidents and experiences that years spent as a city-dweller had all but obliterated. The simple reaction of the kitten to the warmth of my hand revived a memory of myself as a small boy who naively believed that his love for animals, birds, flowers and trees would somehow serve to protect them. I'd thought that by cherishing 'Nature' in all its forms I could conserve it. I had not thought about such things for many years but, lately, these childhood feelings had started to resurface, inspired no doubt by my rural surroundings.

Images from the past flooded my mind as, with my finger and thumb, I gently stroked the body of the black kitten and waited for the vet to return. Best remembered were the days of my childhood spent in the woods and fields by the River Derwent and at the lake at Axwell Park

Estate where I was born. Out of nowhere came the memory of the hurt I felt when I fell out with my best friend, Billy Morrison, as we explored Winlaton Woods because he wanted to take some eggs from a blue-tit's nest we'd found in a hollowed oak tree and I wouldn't let him. I also recalled the shock one Sunday morning of finding a mallard duck flapping about in the meadow grass with half her wing shot away by the irresponsible hunters out for a morning's 'sport'. Like the poet Wordsworth, I had always loved nature and now, at twenty-nine years of age, living a bachelor existence and working in a country market town, these feelings were crystallizing into what was becoming a devotion to the wild creatures and landscapes of Northumberland.

It was 1966 and I had been given the opportunity to work as a lecturer in Educational Studies at Alnwick College of Education in Northumberland. Consequently, I had bought Owl Cottage, an eighteenth-century stone building which stood on a hillside above the River Coquet, with uninterrupted views across the village of Felton towards the distant Cheviot Hills. This was to be a new beginning, the fulfilment of a dream. In the past cats had always been a part of my life and the households of my childhood and youth were never without at least one cat. I loved them all, not least for their dignified and independent natures. Every one of them had been a friend and playmate and every one of them was special. Cats have always fascinated me because they are so mysterious and difficult to analyse in spite of their domesticity.

I knew that cats probably first became domesticated in Ancient Egypt, about 15,000 years ago. For a time cats were even adored as representatives of gods, and their images were sculpted in precious metals encrusted with jewels. Once, on a working trip to Trinity College, Dublin, I was intrigued to find an illustration of a cat in the historic *Book of Kells*, the illuminated manuscript made by the monks on the island of Iona in the eighth or ninth century. Fascinated by this reference I bought a replica bronze statuette of the cat. On the back of the statuette I found the following inscription: 'Cats are both homely and mysterious. They walk silently, mate noisily, they rid us of pests. Their eyes shine in the dark and their pupils change as the moon, from round to crescent. They are sacred to the Moon-goddess and familiars of the feminine.'

For me, cats have always been more than just domesticated animals. They have the 'Call of the Wild', which makes them forsake the comfort of their home from time to time to prowl and hunt, preferably in the fields and woods, but also in our gardens, streets and parks. These characteristics fascinate people across the world to the extent that, for many, keeping cats as pets becomes an addiction.

With these thoughts and sentiments running through my

head I suddenly felt an urge, almost an obligation, to do something even if it seemed reckless as well as hopeless. At this point Mac, having done his deed of mercy with the grey tabby, returned to deal similarly with the two kittens. On a sudden impulse, and to Mac's utter consternation, I scooped up the black-and-white kitten from the table and deposited him carefully into the pocket of my sheepskin jacket.

'You're a sentimental fool,' he said sternly, shocked by my action. 'The wee thing will suffer and die no matter what you do.'

'Well,' I replied, 'he might just as well die in front of my fire as anywhere else. Please send me the bill.'

With these hurried words of farewell I left an incredulous Mac shaking his head.

His words rang in my ears. 'Sentimental fool,' he'd said. How well I recalled the many times those words had been directed towards me, even by my own father, because of my passionate feelings for wildlife. Struggling with these emotions, I drove slowly home on the snow-packed roads and reflected on the harrowing events of the day.

The trip to the vet had followed what began as a normal, dull, grey January day. As I arrived home from work and got out of the car, I felt a heaviness in the air. Living in the country away from the enclosed life of the city had made me far more aware of changes in the weather. By noting how the sky looked, the direction and strength of the wind, as well as the behaviour of birds and animals, my more experienced eye could forecast fairly accurately if any major changes in the weather were on the way.

'It will snow tonight,' a neighbour remarked as he walked his dog along the footpath past my drive.

'Looks like a storm's coming,' I called back.

He smiled and nodded in reply as he was tugged along by Butch, his massive black Labrador. Later, when it did snow, it was heavier than either of us expected.

After closing the garage doors I paused by the tall cypress tree to watch the flocks of crows wheeling noisily over their rookery, having returned from marauding the local fields. I loved to watch the sky at this time of day when the soft gentle light of evening slowly gave way to darkness. Sometimes there would be such a subtle toning of colours that the landscape looked like a Turner painting. Alone in my garden at such a moment I could indulge the thought that this was a private viewing for my eyes only. On other days, the colours of sunset would be so boldly red, orange and yellow that they mesmerized me with their beauty. I often reflected that I never had enough time just to watch and appreciate the sky. Tonight, though, there was no sunset – only overcast clouds that gave off a half-light.

As I dawdled, the air all around grew still and became electric. I stood spellbound, aware that something eventful was about to happen. Then it began to grow darker and I felt a sudden chill. Snow started to fall silently, driving the chaffinches and blackbirds from the bird-table to seek sanctuary in the hedges that fringed the wood at the end of my garden. Despite the cold, I stayed there for a few more moments, witnessing the first snowfall of winter. Suddenly, the tranquil scene changed dramatically and I was nearly swept off my feet by sudden gusts of wind that turned the shower into a blizzard. Covered in huge flakes of snow and numbed with cold, I hastily made for the patio door of the cottage.

Once inside, I felt besieged by the storm which was growing stronger by the minute. It rattled the back door and covered the window panes with pale shutters of snow. I shed my overcoat, brushing it free of snowflakes, and hung it to dry in the narrow hall. The sounds of the gale outside grew wilder but this only added to my feelings of safety and comfort inside the cottage. It was Friday and the weekend beckoned with its promise of rest and recreation. Icy draughts from the doors and windows swept around me but failed to dampen my good spirits as I put a match to the log fire and lit the candles around the sitting room. After a hot meal of grilled steak and fried potatoes, I settled down by the fireside with a book and a glass of wine for an evening of homely bliss. I was as yet unaware of the coming turn of events that would shatter my relaxation and change my life for many years to come.

The mellow chimes of the French clock striking seven awoke me from an armchair snooze. By this time the storm had moved on and I became aware of an all-pervading stillness. The fire had burned down to roasting hot embers that warmed me right through to my toes and my armchair was, at that moment, the most comfortable place in the whole world. But the particular quiet that comes after a storm is alluring and I couldn't resist the temptation to look outside and sample the night air. The view from my back doorway was bleak but breathtaking. The windblown snow had transformed the familiar scene into a wilderness of pure white. It felt bitterly cold and the air tasted dry and frosted like chilled wine. The sky had cleared and a full moon shone starkly down from a black background of shimmering stars unlike anything I ever saw in the polluted skies of the cities where I had lived for so many years. It thrilled me to imagine again that perhaps I was a solitary witness to this splendour. As far as I could see from my back door, none of my neighbours were sharing the beauty of this night. It was a Christmas-card scene so captivating that it held me there until I realized I was slowly beginning to freeze. I moved to return indoors.

Suddenly, the silence was pierced by the scream of an animal. It was a strident cry of pain, totally shattering the stillness that had followed the heavy snowfall. It was frightening and terrible to hear and in the midst of all the beauty around me it seemed so unreal. I felt as if every sense in my body was switched to full alert. Shocked and alarmed, I strained to find out where it came from. Then I heard it again, a howl full of agony and distress. It sounded close by but I could see nothing. It came again and yet again. This time I thought I knew roughly the location it was coming from. Moving out to get a better view I found myself having to wade through powdery snowdrifts, slipping and sliding in my haste. In spite of shivering in the intense cold I pressed on without a thought for my inadequate clothing. I didn't have a coat on and I was only wearing my carpet slippers. Eventually, I reached the outskirts of the wood that led to Blackbrook Farm. Something squirmed in the snow ahead and wailed with the torment of moving. A silver-grey cat lay twisting and turning in a gin-trap which held it fast by the hind leg.

As I approached, the cat's struggles to escape became frenzied and I saw that the snow around it was heavily bloodstained. Shocked and distressed by the sight, I had to find a way to release it, but that proved far from easy. Demented by its injuries and panicked by my presence, it hindered my well-intentioned efforts with a fit of spitting and clawing. Scrambling about on my hands and knees in the snow, I eventually succeeded in prising open the jaws of the rusty trap which had bitten deeply into its leg. To my surprise, despite its severe wounds, the cat took off at high speed through the snow and was quickly gone from sight. Breathless with exertion and badly scratched and bitten about the hands and arms, I struggled to find a footing on the frozen ground but managed to raise myself up. Still reeling from the shock of this sudden and unexpected experience, at first I didn't know what I should do, if anything. Where had the cat gone? Had it simply headed for the nearest cover? Was it now lying under some fir tree, racked with pain? Cold and wet, I decided to return to the cottage for comfort and medication, as well as time to think. A welcome glass of brandy, some first aid and a roasting in front of the revived log fire did much to restore my spirits.

As I thawed out I reviewed the situation. Thinking about what I had seen started to vex me. It was worrying to think about the injured cat and how desperately it needed help. 'I can't just leave things like that,' I said to myself aloud, but it wasn't really any business of mine. Perhaps I should leave it alone. After all, it was getting late and I was tired. Also, it wasn't the weather to go tramping around looking for an injured animal and either a fox or farm dog would most probably have got to it already. Even if the cat survived until daylight, the carrion crows, nature's scavengers, would soon dispatch it and that would be the end of it. Still, I had spent a childhood living with cats and I had a great fondness for them. It was an irritating dilemma for me but after only a short tussle my conscience won the day and I resolved to try to track and find the cat. What I would do then was a matter for future consideration. Quickly fortifying myself with my sheepskin jacket, the thickest gloves I could find and Wellington boots, I armed myself with a walking stick and set off in pursuit before I could change my mind.

The cat's paw tracks in the snow were easy enough to pick out by the light of the moon, especially where they were spattered with blood. Under the trees it was harder to see the tracks, particularly as they meandered through a dense clump of blackthorn and sometime later through a plantation of young firs. I floundered through packed snow, breathing hard, as the trail plunged down a sharp incline. I slithered and fell as I tried to find it again after it had disappeared through an overgrown drainage ditch. Sweating profusely and already exhausted, I wondered where the cat was going: surely it should have given up by now. Abruptly, the tracks turned almost at a right angle as the cat headed, to my relief, over open country. This animal had a definite purpose in mind but I puzzled over what it could be. Tired and out of breath, I was already feeling that I'd had enough. I decided that if I didn't find it soon, I would turn back for home.

The trail suddenly became more direct and appeared to head for a tumbledown barn in the near distance. I had to marvel at this animal's stamina, especially in places where it had literally dragged itself through the snow. It was hard enough for me to walk as I kept sliding and losing balance on the freezing ground.

Soon I was standing inside the opening of the derelict building. At first it was hard to see anything in the darkness, but after a time my eyes adjusted to the gloom. With the help of the moonlight reflecting off the snow outside, I began to search the darker corners where I thought a wounded cat might go. I had no luck there. Mystified, I started to examine the walls of the separate stalls because I thought a cat could perhaps climb up into a corner or some other hiding place that wasn't easy to see from the ground. At last, I found a pathway of bloodspots which traced the cat's passage to where a broken door gave access to an inner shed. The door had seen better days and I was easily able to wrench it open, but there was nothing inside except a rusty corn bin and some straw. I regretted not bringing a torch. Through holes in the timbers I could see that it had begun snowing again. The wind blew flakes of it through the gaps against my face and clothing as I searched around. It felt bitterly cold even in the shelter of the barn and I could feel a chill on my back from the cold sweat of my shirt. I worried that the search was probably foolhardy, but I was determined to persevere for a little while longer.

There was no sign of the cat anywhere but a closer

inspection of the wall around a warped wooden shelf revealed more spots of blood and a well-defined route of scratch marks leading upwards. Judging from the signs I'd seen, the cat was bleeding badly and possibly wouldn't last much longer without help. It could be anywhere in the roof area and it probably wouldn't be safe for me to go up there even if I somehow managed the climb. Then I remembered that when I came in I'd noticed a ladder lying near the entrance to the barn.

Hurrying back to the front of the building I found the wooden ladder half-buried in dirt. Pulling it free I saw that two rungs were missing. It looked to be in a poor state but I thought it might be worth giving it a try. Quickly propping the ladder up against the wall where I believed the cat had climbed, I found it reached right up to where there was a sort of hatchway into the roof. The ladder must have been used in the past to gain access to a hay store in the loft. The hatchway didn't look too high so I thought I'd chance it. If I still couldn't find the cat after this effort, then I'd go home.

I cautiously inched my way up the rickety ladder. I was now more than ever determined to see this thing through to the end. I am not that keen on heights at the best of times but by now I knew that what I was doing was madly reckless. What if I fell and broke a leg? Would anybody find me? In spite of these acute anxieties, I continued to climb.

Pushing and shoving my way up against dusty, cobwebbed

timbers, I eased myself between the rotting planks and crawled out on to the floor above. Remnants of straw and hay were strewn all around and the impression I had was that everything was in a state of near collapse. Towards the rear end of the loft there was an opening to the outside, with a patch of windblown snow around it. Possibly this had once been a loading bay. Bird-droppings littered part of the flooring and looking up I could just make out the shapes of last summer's swallow nests. Shafts of moonlight seeped through the gaps between the sprung timbers of the roof and softly illumined the dark-beamed joists and warped floorboards of the loft stretching out before me. The question was, where had the cat gone?

As I slowly looked around I heard a wet licking sound which drew me to a corner where, amid the debris of leaves and straw, the silver-grey cat had come to rest. Not wishing to alarm it in any way and mindful of its claws, I cautiously approached and, from a safe distance, peered into the recess. Was this its den? Had it crawled here to die as badly wounded wild animals have been known to do? As I edged slowly closer, a moonbeam slanted through a hole in the roof and momentarily lit up the corner. I realized that I had been witness to the most powerful of all instincts in the animal kingdom. The silver-grey cat was a mother, driven by the maternal instinct to return to succour her two kittens. In front of me, a rough nest had been scraped together for her family. Not trusting the loose timbers to accommodate my weight while standing, I crawled nearer on hands and knees until I was at last able to inspect the family by the dim moonlight.

They were a pitiful sight. The kittens, as far as I could see were at most only a couple of weeks old and merely frail bundles of skin and bone covered in ragged fur. They hardly seemed to move at all, despite the she-cat's insistent licking as she worked feverishly to caress some life into them. They had obviously been left on their own for some considerable time. I stared aghast at what I'd found and it filled me with despair. The she-cat seemed oblivious to her own plight, determined to mother her kittens at all costs. Perhaps it was already too late, but I felt I had to make the effort to seek help for them, especially after making it this far.

Transporting them was more easily accomplished than I'd expected. I found a remnant of sacking, dusty with chaff and seed husks but dry and warm nonetheless. The she-cat watched me, wide-eyed and strangely gentle, as I carefully lifted her mangled body on to the sacking, followed by the tiny, frail kittens. She must have been in great pain as I moved her but all the fight and fear appeared to have bled out of her and she was content now that she was back with her kittens. There were a few anxious moments when I came to descend the ladder but, apart from a number of painfully bruising jolts, I succeeded in reaching the floor of the barn without mishap. From there I hurried home by a more direct and, I hoped, easier route than the one by which I'd come.

The ground outside was frozen hard and I found myself stumbling and skidding with the effort of carrying the cat and her kittens over frozen patches of snow and ice. I was more worried about their safety than my own and a couple of times I lost my balance and thudded down, saving them from dropping at the expense of falling hard. I was beginning to ache in places that I'd forgotten I had.

At one point I decided to cross a field in order to shorten the journey but it proved to be a time-consuming mistake. I found myself struggling through deep drifts and stumbling over concealed stones and other debris. Nevertheless, I kept going as fast as the deep snow and the care of my charges would allow.

I reached the cottage almost on the point of collapse. Even though I was feeling physically worn-out and emotionally drained, I wasted no time and began to summon help. It was just after 9 p.m.; the whole episode had taken a mere two hours yet it seemed an eternity since I had been relaxing in front of the fire. Directory Enquiries gave me a number to telephone and soon the three casualties were safe in the boot of my car as I drove as fast as conditions would allow, along roads covered in snow, to the local veterinary clinic in Alnwick. Their fate would soon be in the hands of a professional and my task, thankfully, would be over. Or so I thought at the time.

Arriving home from the vet's some two hours later with the sole remaining kitten still, hopefully, warm and safe in my pocket, I felt weakened and fatigued by the evening's turn of events. It had all happened so quickly that it was difficult for me to fully comprehend that it really had occurred. The cottage was warm and friendly in contrast to the brutal weather outside and after the disappointment of losing the mother cat and her kitten, it was uplifting to feel the comfort of familiar surroundings again.

Gingerly, I removed the surviving kitten from my pocket and placed him with great care on to a woollen rug near the fire. At first I couldn't tell whether he was alive or not but suddenly the tiny creature sneezed, probably due to the dust in my pocket. It was at that moment I realized the enormity of the task that lay ahead of me. Here I was, expected to play nursemaid to a little wild animal that was only about two-weeks old and barely alive. I was totally inexperienced for this task and suddenly felt quite inadequate. What had I been thinking of to get myself into such a predicament?

The odds against me having any chance at all of rearing the kitten successfully were too far-fetched to even consider. But all my efforts throughout this evening had been motivated by feelings of compassion for a badly injured cat that, as it turned out, had been killed by human cruelty. I had brought the surviving kitten home as an act of mercy, rather than having it put to death, but I hadn't thought it through. I began to reflect that possibly I had been too impulsive. Nevertheless, as it was a problem of my own making I would just have to do what I could in the circumstances.

I was reminded of times past when, as a boy, I'd gone fishing for minnows only to find that my catch couldn't survive captivity in a jam jar. So I would trek back to the lake to set them free again. This felt like a similar situation except that this time I could not face the humiliation of taking the kitten back to the vet.

After a recuperative mug of tea and a short spell by the fireside, I felt in a better mood to tackle the problem. Anyway, I thought, the creature will probably pass away any minute now. The image of the injured she-cat returned to haunt me. I was suffering from feelings of guilt towards the kitten on behalf of my fellow humans who had killed his mother. As a lover of wild creatures and the countryside I know that gamekeepers and hunters use various trapping devices against animal life in the fields and woods, but I think the practice of using gin-traps is particularly wicked. Aimed at safeguarding flocks of pheasants and grouse so that the landed gentry and their guests can shoot them down in mid-August, it causes the deaths of innocent victims. Unsuspecting animals, such as rabbits, weasels, pine martens, foxes and badgers, who step on the trap release a spring holding back serrated iron jaws which trap the animal's foot. Many creatures have been known to bite through their ensnared limb in order to escape, only to die later from blood loss or an infection; others, such as the mother cat, writhe in awful agony and face a slow and pain-filled death. Since that fateful night when the silver-grey cat died, I have made it my business to destroy gin-traps wherever I find them on my country walks.

My immediate and most pressing problem was what I could do to successfully rear this pathetic little creature, a true orphan of the storm. Whenever in my life I have been uncertain about what to do, I have found the best answer is to actually do something straightaway, but without panicking, and to think about it in depth later. I wanted to avoid making a terrible mistake, though: there was a life at stake here.

Grabbing the poker I wrestled the dying fire into an all-warming blaze. Then I embarked upon a course of action. I knew that the kitten needed to be fed as soon as possible. I remembered that somewhere in a copy of *Reader's Digest* I'd read an account of a woman who'd reared an abandoned litter of puppies who were only a few weeks old. Initially, she'd fed them by using a fountain pen to squeeze a kind of milky mixture into their mouths. Surely, I said to myself, I must have an old fountain pen somewhere. Hurriedly searching through the congested rubbish in the drawers of my desk I retrieved an old Swan fountain pen. In great haste, I flushed out the dried ink sac and removed the pen nib. From the limited resources available to me, I filled the ink sac with some tinned evaporated milk which I fortified with halibut oil squeezed from a gelatine capsule. Next, I heated the mixture by immersing it briefly in a cup of warm water. I hoped that the kitten would accept this milky concoction.

I had never held any living thing which was as fragile as this. Holding the tiny body firmly, I gently opened the diminutive mouth with two of my fingers and, taking the pen sac in my other hand, I squeezed some of the milky solution into its mouth. The resulting reaction was both explosive and at the same time reassuring. The formerly dormant and almost lifeless body went into a convulsion of spluttering and gasping and then a minute pink tongue emerged to the accompaniment of gasps and wheezes. At least the little thing is still alive, I thought as I continued to squeeze some liquid into the tiny mouth. Gaining confidence from this show of life, I set about completing what his late lamented mother had started when I found her.

First of all, I cleaned the kitten all over. With cotton wool buds soaked in warm water I washed it down and cut away the matted tufts from its sparse fur coat. As all cat lovers know, for cats washing is not only routine care, it is a way of life and I hoped what I was doing would be therapeutic. Soon, I noticed that the kitten's body had begun to tremble and quiver all over with barely audible sneezes and snorting noises as if its whole being was coming alive again. Wet and dishevelled-looking after its bed bath, it presented an endearing picture of frailty and baby-animal innocence.

There were bald patches on its head, hind parts and stomach, while its eyes were gummed shut with semi-hardened pus. In the gentlest way I could, I nursed the little being and then became afraid to do any more in case the attention caused it to go into remission and die on me. Using a hairdryer on a low setting, I dried it as best I could. Then placing it very carefully in front of the fire in a cardboard box lined with a blanket, I retired to my bed, weary and worn out by all the effort and worry of a dramatic night. I slipped at once into a relaxed doze, consoled by the thought that I'd done all I could for the kitten.

As I drifted off I mused upon my emotions which were already becoming attached to this little creature. I had saved it from what was almost certain death twice. Firstly, by freeing its mother from the trap and, secondly, by preventing the vet from putting it down because its chances of survival without a mother were nil. It began to register in my sleepy mind that I had accepted a challenge which would require enormous luck as well as determination and effort. And then it dawned upon me that I was no longer thinking of the kitten as an 'it' but as a 'him'. Too tired to think anymore, I slipped into a deep sleep.

Fortunately, the following day was Saturday which I would normally spend at home. In view of last night's adventures, this was to prove fortunate in the kitten's struggle for survival. As soon as I awoke I remembered everything that had transpired the night before with startling clarity. I wanted to rush out of bed immediately and check that the kitten had not died during the night. I didn't, though, because I was scared of what I might find. As I lay in bed worrying I began to think negative thoughts like those I'd had the night before regarding the immensity of the task facing me. For one thing I very much enjoyed leading an independent life with as few ties and commitments as possible. Having a sick kitten to look after would certainly intrude upon my space and freedom. And ideally the little creature needed good nurturing from his mother for at least another month. 'Face reality!' I told myself. But the she-cat was no longer with us and I had impulsively, but nonetheless willingly, taken responsibility for at least trying to salvage something worthwhile from the tragedy. It was therefore my job to see it through to some kind of satisfactory conclusion. Resolving to deal sensibly with whatever I would find downstairs, I got out of bed.

There are many advantages to living in an ancient stone cottage with walls which are almost three feet thick. One of these is the insulation from the world outside, not only in terms of sound but also temperature. On the hottest days of summer the inside of the cottage is pleasantly cool, shielded by the thick stone walls from the heat outside. In winter the reverse is true as the heat from the fire is retained by those very same stone walls. Downstairs was still warm from yesterday's fire, giving it a homely atmosphere.

Apprehensively, I approached the box in which I'd placed the kitten. At first I couldn't see him but on closer inspection there he lay: a coiled mite of fur with only the slightest body movements which I took to be his breathing. I felt rewarded beyond my wildest hopes but knew it was too early to expect that everything would be alright.

Feeling really happy, I set about restoring the cottage to good order and soon the fire was blazing and the smell of coffee and grilled bacon filled the air so that everything felt cosy and warm, in sharp contrast to the wintry scenes outdoors. Overnight the weather had grown more severe and temperatures had dropped below freezing. Later, when I replenished the bird-table with the breakfast leftovers, the thermometer near the birdbath read -5°C. Opening the front door to collect the milk required a supreme effort because the windblown snow had frozen and sealed the door edges to the frame during the night. It also required

The silver she-cat had raked together a rough nest of straw for her two kittens.

He looked the picture of a miniature Toby Jug, and that would now have to be his name.

As a special treat I drove down to the beach for a view of Lindisfarne.

The tomato thief exposed for all to see.

a big effort to free the bottles from the ice which held them fast. The milkman must have had a superhuman struggle to deliver the milk at all. I was most thankful for his toil.

The open porch had been transformed overnight into an ice house, festooned with long icicles sparkling in the morning sun. Inspecting the frozen bottles of milk I saw that the blue tits had been there before me and had pecked neat little holes in the silver tops. Nearby, in a stand of pine trees across the road, a pair of magpies chittered in annoyance at me. Obviously, they also had their eyes on the milk.

The wintry scenery was breathtaking in its beauty but piercingly cold. The trees drooped under heavy garlands of snow. In addition there was an otherworldliness about everything, cloaked as it was in arctic white. The sound of the traffic was muffled as were the cries of the children sledging on the snowbanks above the river, a happy reminder of my own childhood in winters past.

Returning indoors, the temptation was to huddle up by the fire with a hot drink and observe the snowy wilderness through the glass of the patio door. Rousing myself from the desire to spend the day cosseted as a 'couch potato' in the armchair by the fireside, I began to address the more immediate problems of rearing the sole survivor of last night's storm.

That day was spent working urgently to save the kitten

from reaching a life-threatening point of no return. I fed him with the fountain pen sac and kept him warm. I washed and cleaned him, stroking him with a cotton wool ball lightly dipped in lukewarm water to mimic his mother's licking and grooming behaviour. During it all I spoke tenderly to him to soothe him and encourage him to live. I did little else but minister to the kitten, even to the point of sitting next to his box, which lay close to the hearth, whilst I was sipping a hot drink. I sat by him, coffee mug in hand, watching him anxiously and speaking to him softly as he slept the day away.

Looking at him as he slept, I was in awe of the capacity of cats to sleep at will and with absolute relaxation. We have created the term 'catnap' to describe the luxury of a short but reviving sleep, often taken in the comfort of a favourite armchair. For cats, sleeping is not only restful but also a healing process and I fervently hoped that was the case for this kitten. Still, healing takes time. This kitten needed time to sleep in safety, as well as warmth, with food and lots of tender loving care. My cottage had been effectively turned into a nursing home to enable this tiny cat to live as a testament not only to his own instinct for survival, but to my adamant refusal to abandon him and, of course, to my commitment to his care.

I told myself all of this as I retired once more to my bed after a final check that the kitten looked to be sleeping peacefully, apart from occasional brief body spasms. I found it difficult to sleep that night and kept waking to tiptoe downstairs to keep the fire going and alleviate my anxiety about the kitten. It was similar, I assumed, to looking after a baby or a sick child and I became aware that I was adopting essentially the role of substitute parent.

As I nursed the kitten through these anxious early days of our life together, I reflected on how Owl Cottage fulfilled a long-held ambition of mine to live in the country after enduring several years in London at the start of my career. It had always been my intention to have a pet, most probably a kitten, as soon as I had a house with a garden. My dream of a house and garden had now become a reality but a pet had not been quite so high on my agenda at that particular moment in time.

Since buying and making my home in Owl Cottage over a year ago I had very much enjoyed living alone but it looked as if fate had taken a hand in my affairs. Out of the blue, I now had another life to consider, albeit one that sadly might cease at any moment. This tiny wild creature in just a few hours had made me realize how empty my home life had been without another living thing to care for. I found that I was rapidly changing my mind about being a completely free agent. Indeed, I was growing to like the thought of having another living creature to share my home with. I began to rejoice in the idea, however challenging, of raising this kitten as a pet.

Sunday morning came with a deep winter look about it. All the window panes were frosted over with what as children we called Jack Frost stars. Downstairs the cottage remained warm and I could see in the dim light that there were traces of glowing embers left amongst the ashes. Soon I had the fire roaring up the chimney, bringing the cottage awake again. Now I had to address the question of caring for this very sick kitten still lying precisely where I'd placed him the night before in the cardboard box. As I lifted him out and cradled him in my hand, he felt just like a tiny bag of bones and I despaired at my lack of common sense in hoping that I could nurse him back to health. Feeding him from the pen tube proved a messy business and I doubted whether he got much into his stomach. It was like holding a lifeless sack and several times I thought he had died, only to be reassured by a cough and what passed for a whimper.

There was no apparent progress that day and the kitten just lay in the box, dormant, in a curved foetal position. I really believed that he was dying but I stubbornly persisted in taking him out every few hours to force some of the milky mixture into him. At times I felt like giving up in frustration and I sensed hopelessness in what I was attempting to do. Sometimes I thought about taking him back to the vet so that he could die in peace. But I didn't and I kept thinking, 'I'll give it one more try,' followed by another and yet another until the whole day passed in a succession of

28

depressing attempts to achieve the impossible, I concluded that nothing short of a miracle was needed, but then miracles sometimes happen.

I felt very much the same on the Monday morning when I had to shake off all of these feelings in order to go back to work. After feeding and washing him I left the kitten, a black lump of fur in the box near the fire, with the feeling that it had all been a waste of time. In fact, it was with immense relief that I sped off to college. I was finding caring extremely hard going. Once there, I didn't tell any of my colleagues about my traumatic weekend because I couldn't face the strong possibility that all my best efforts to save the kitten were doomed to failure. Now that I was away from the cottage and my patient, I was back in the real world in which the childish fantasy of rearing a sickly, half-dead kitten was farcical even to my mind. With a sinking heart I drove slowly home at the end of the day, afraid at what I might find, with a part of me hoping he had died and so released me from emotional torment.

There had been another heavy snowfall during the afternoon and I had great difficulty negotiating the driveway to the garage. The cottage assumed a dark and gloomy aspect in keeping with my mood. I even wondered whether I should walk down the bank to the Northumberland Arms for a bite to eat and some alcohol to drown my sorrows at what might be waiting for me inside the cottage. I stood for several moments outside, considering this option and staring up at the myriad of stars in the vastness of space above me. Normally, this night-time view of the universe served to raise my spirits but tonight it did nothing for me. Perhaps, I decided, it would be best to see what the situation was first and then go to the pub afterwards. Forcing myself to put the key in the lock, I went inside. I thought let's do a quick check and then get out. I imagined that I'd find a stiff little body already in the throes of rigor mortis. Refusing to put on the lights, I shone a torch I'd taken from the boot of the car directly into the kitten's box.

The sight that greeted me was truly amazing. Instead of finding him lying dead the kitten must have heard me come in and was shuffling around, making what I assumed to be squeaks of hunger. Overcome with happiness at this development, I yanked off my coat and set to work with renewed optimism. I was filled with joy at finding him alive in spite of my worst fears. I never did get to the local pub that night. This creature was hanging in there with all the tenacity Mother Nature had endowed him with and it was truly wondrous to witness.

Two days later a further crisis developed. When I returned from work I found the kitten convulsing with chesty coughs. His nose and mouth were covered in phlegm and there was more pus around his eyes, which had still failed to open. Sick at heart, I coldly reviewed the situation. His condition was ultra serious, it was probably some form of influenza, possibly pneumonia or pleurisy. It might even be cat flu which I'd heard was almost incurable. Whatever it was I considered it likely to be fatal. This small creature could not keep on going against such odds. What should I do? I suddenly felt totally weary of it all, too weary to bother to take him to Mac's for the inevitable. I decided that I would continue to do everything I could for the little fellow and, if he did have to die, it would be on my lap.

Then a strange thing happened to me, something which I couldn't ever remember happening before: I began to weep uncontrollably. Much later, my feelings eased somewhat. Resigning myself to whatever might lie ahead, I began to deal with the situation as positively as possible.

Of course, I did what I could to treat his condition but I did it without hope. I bathed his face, and cleaned his nostrils and his mouth. I squeezed fresh orange juice into a cup and soaking the end of a cotton handkerchief in it, I dripped some into his open mouth so that he would get the vitamin C. I'd read somewhere that this was what people did in the olden days to unblock the throats of children who were dying of diphtheria. And all the while my tears flowed as my feelings overwhelmed me.

I had already grown to love this creature and I couldn't bear the thought of losing him now. I had put a huge emotional investment into trying to save the kitten and looking down at him I felt as if it had all been for nothing. He lay limply in my hand except when the coughing convulsed him. All night long I continued these ministrations. It was important to me that I gave him as much comfort as possible because it was through my arrogance in believing that I could save him that he was suffering now. I wouldn't let him die alone. Sometime later during the night I forced a quarter of an aspirin into him. Then, exhausted, I fell asleep sitting in the chair, with the kitten on a towel in my lap.

I awakened feeling stiff and cold. It was just after six o'clock in the morning and still dark outside. The kitten still lay where I'd put him. He felt warm and had stopped coughing. I placed him in his box and then I loaded and stoked the fire into roasting flames. I needed to shave and shower as soon it would be time to leave for work. After a cup of tea I attended my patient. He was still alive but there was a sickly aura about him. I fed him and washed him as best I could. All the sorrow of the previous night had left me drained and I felt much relieved as if my tears had washed away the residue of tension which had accumulated since the rescue. It was again a relief to go to work for a brief respite but he was on my mind all day.

The next few days seem in retrospect to blend into one another as I continued to care for the kitten. I spent all my time at home looking after him. If I read or wrote anything it was always close to where I could see and hear him. Fortunately, there were no more crises.

When I checked him on Saturday morning there appeared to be a change. Somehow, he looked different. It was perhaps the way he was lying in his box. No longer was he lying on his side in a huddled curve, rather he was upright in a more typical cat-like position with feet and paws tucked under him like a nesting hen, although I must say, a very tiny hen. When I lifted him he mewed softly. Could he possibly be on the mend? Adrenaline rushed through me and filled me with the excitement of new hope. This put a fresh vista on everything. I felt happy for the first time in days and everything around me seemed brighter and better. I was more than ever determined to do whatever was necessary to save this kitten if I could.

From appearances the kitten seemed little changed but at least now when I fed him, amidst the splutters and snorts, there seemed to be a relishing of the milky concoction. I thought I could just detect a very tiny tongue-licking action with what I interpreted as enthusiasm, albeit faint, but nonetheless there. His eyes were still gummed shut and the grey bald patches on his skin showed no signs of improvement but intuitively I could sense that this little fellow was putting up a tremendous fight for his life.

Optimistically, I began to believe that together there might be a chance for us to beat the odds. The only time that I wasn't occupied doing things either for the kitten or myself was when I was dozing into sleep and this was when I had the time to think. This kitten's fight to live was testament to the enduring ability of living things to recover and adapt in the face of hardship if given help, support and, perhaps, some luck. Just before I fell asleep I had come to the conclusion that the kitten had been extremely lucky. And, furthermore, so had I. Tomorrow would tell, I believed, whether or not he really was on the mend. For the first time in several days I looked forward happily to the next morning.

Kittens grow up fast and two days in the life of a kitten is a long time compared to a human, so I was hoping to see a definite improvement in the condition of the kitten after a whole weekend of intensive care and nurture. As it turned out, I was not to be disappointed.

On Monday morning I arose bright and early to see how things were. The kitten lay coiled in a little fluffy ball, snuggled into the blanket in a corner of his box. No sign of life greeted me until I lifted him out and placed him gently on to a hand towel on my lap. He didn't seem strong enough yet to stand and he appeared very fragile. Holding him in my hand I attempted to feed him from the pen sac, only this time it wouldn't work. Inserting the business end of the sac into his tiny mouth, which as usual I had prised open, I squeezed carefully and nothing happened. I squeezed harder and the sac burst, spraying the evaporated milk mixture over the kitten, the kitchen table and my clothes. I suppose the fountain pen ink sac had never been intended for this purpose, although it had so far done sterling service.

I considered what I could do now as I cleaned up the mess. I resorted to ladling the milk directly into his mouth using a miniature silver-plated sugar spoon found abandoned in the cutlery drawer. I vaguely remembered it among the many keepsakes I had from my grandmother's house. It seemed perfect for the job. The reaction to the first spoonful was discouraging. There was a great deal of spitting and snorting but some of the milk obviously went down. The second and third offerings caused him to gulp and gasp for breath but he didn't choke, although at times it seemed as if he would. When I felt he'd had enough, I sponged his face and chest which were by this time extremely messy.

It was then that I noticed the bald patches on his skin had become red and looked really sore. I decided to apply some Evening Primrose ointment that my mother had given me to heal my hands after I'd been doing some building work. I had never used it and it took me a while to remember where I'd stored it. It was to prove very useful and I applied the sticky ointment with great care to the kitten's bald patches. During these ministrations he simply lay quietly on the towel in my lap and seemed to be soothed into sleep by my fingers gently stroking the balm into his skin. He had a most affable temperament, even allowing for his weakened state. I was beginning to appreciate that there was something very special about this little cat, something simply lovable. Day by day he seemed to be developing and changing for the better.

As the week went on and his health continued to improve, I had another problem. Since the kitten appeared to be progressing so well I worried what would happen if he became really active and escaped his box. Cats, even kittens, are exceptionally good climbers so my worries about him in this respect were not unfounded. I also needed to make sure that the kitten wouldn't die of hypothermia in an old draughty cottage when the fire went out. I expected that his immune system couldn't cope with any more of a battering than he'd so far endured.

It was a freezing Thursday morning and I was preparing to go to work but the problem nagged at my mind. After giving the matter serious consideration, I took a clear, wide-bottomed glass jug, which usually contained dried flowers, from the bathroom and some cotton-wool balls which I used whenever I cut myself shaving. Putting the two together offered the ideal solution. Emptying the jug, washing and drying it, I covered the bottom with cotton wool and stood it on an old-fashioned, three-legged stool called a cracket which I'd inherited from my grandmother. Then I moved the cracket closer to the fire. Next, I very carefully lifted the kitten and placed him gently in the centre of the cotton-wool base. Whilst I was away he could be as active as he liked but the jug would ensure that he was kept warm. Now I felt I could happily leave him in safety and comfort. I wished I'd thought of it sooner.

Since the morning weather report on the radio predicted a further sharp fall in temperature for the rest of the day, I stoked the fire as fully as I could and drew the curtains to make the room as cosy as possible. With a last look at the tiny figure I hurriedly, but reluctantly, left for work. While the kitten still required 'Intensive Care', at last the situation was easing down from 'Critical' to the 'Patient is Comfortable and Out of Danger'.

After a hectic and frustrating day at work, I drove into the driveway of the cottage and anxiously let myself in through the patio door. My small living room felt warm and cosy in contrast to how desperately cold it was outside. There was a faint red glow from the burned-down fire and in the subdued light from a table lamp I examined the contents of the jug. Gently, I felt inside and touched the dark ball of fluff almost cocooned within the cotton-wool lining and to my utter relief it stirred. He was alive and seemed well. This event, however small in its cosmic significance, caused me immense satisfaction and I hastened to bring the cottage alive once more with heat, light, food and music.

This pattern of events became the routine for the rest of

that week. Although there were some anxious moments, I gradually came to realize that the kitten was likely to survive. I even felt sure that the kitten had grown bigger in his time with me. Whenever I fed him now, his body appeared to be firmer and he seemed less devoted to sleeping than previously. Several times I noticed him shuffling around in the jug as if he was trying to assert his right to an active life.

There were a number of high spots during the next week to balance out the worrisome times. There was the morning when, after feeding him and bathing his face, he at last opened his eyes and looked at me with what seemed like two tiny blue jewels. The memory of that moment, of the look of wonder and bemusement on his grizzled face at seeing me and the world around him for the very first time, caused me to break into a chuckle whenever I thought about it for the rest of the day.

Then there was the time four weeks after finding him that I came home from work to an amusing and, as it proved, eventful sight. As I came into the room the kitten's diminutive figure was raised on hind legs, peering out from the inside of the jug as if to welcome me. For some days he had been responding to me more and more. He seemed to be increasingly aware of my presence whenever I came near him and his body would turn to face the direction of my voice whenever I spoke to him.

I needed to give him a name.

Watching him as carefully as I did I saw that he was developing into an extremely interesting personality. I was impressed by the way he shuffled around his jug as he negotiated the lumps of cotton wool with fierce determination. And then there was the way he would peer through the thick glass sides of the jug as he sought to make some sense of his world. Watching him, I was fascinated and I believed his progress to be nothing short of miraculous.

The sight of him in the jug that evening clinched an appropriate name for him. No other name would be so right. He looked the picture of a miniature Toby Jug as he stood peering out through the glass and from now on that would be his name: he would be known always as Toby Jug no matter what else happened. This decision also settled something else that had been hovering in my mind – the uncertainty of whether he would or would not survive. Now I was filled with a firm sense of conviction that the kitten I'd rescued on that foul night over four weeks ago was, against all the odds, going to live. It seemed a lifetime since I'd brought him home and I really hadn't expected then that he would survive. But here he was, alive and kicking, and very much emerging as a personality with which to be reckoned.

Some days later, Toby Jug surprised me yet again with his accelerating health and his burgeoning instinct for survival.

I was still feeding him from the small spoon which was now known as 'Toby Jug's spoon'. While I was spooning the milky concoction into him I noticed that he was beginning to lick the spoon. Two or three feeds later I observed him not only licking at the spoon but actually licking the top of my hand where some of the milk had spilled. This was progress indeed and the next step was to see whether he could lap directly from a saucer.

The first experiments were total failures. At this stage, Toby Jug was still extremely small, if not to say minute. In comparison to his size, saucers proved quite large and far too high for him to reach over to lap the milk. Back to square one. I continued feeding him with the spoon until a few days later when I happened to be shopping in a Woolworths store.

On one of the displays I spotted a children's play-pack of miniature place-settings for a doll's house. I thought the saucers looked just the right size for Toby Jug and bought one on the spot. Hastening home, I couldn't wait to try it out.

Toby was confused at first and couldn't work out what was expected of him. So I raised the saucer with the milk to his mouth and, holding him steady with the other hand, I gently nudged his face into the liquid. He gasped and spluttered as he usually did when I fed him, but as I persevered Toby gradually got the message. Finally, there was no stopping him as he attacked the milk in the saucer with gusto. Yet another major step along the road to recovery, I thought.

'Bright little cat,' I said, watching him, but by then Toby was experiencing the first principle of cat lore: 'Be Independent'. The determination he showed in the way he shoved his face into that saucer of milk revealed his true mettle. It meant the past was behind him and Toby Jug was here to stay. I know that some people disapprove of giving milk to cats in the belief that it can give them constipation and make them ill, but the cats I have known have all been supremely healthy and happy animals who thrive on drinking milk, the creamier the better. In Toby Jug's case, I needed to duplicate the health-sustaining properties of a mother cat's milk and the concoction of unsweetened evaporated milk with an added booster of halibut oil proved to be a life-saver. However, he also needed to drink water so from then on he had both, although the milk mixture continued to be a firm favourite at this point in time.

From that Saturday onwards there was no holding him back. Toby rapidly advanced to semi-solid foods, which I bought for him at the supermarket as I didn't have any type of food processor. I purchased baby foods for him at first. Any meat with vegetables was favoured but he especially appreciated the milky puddings. However, Toby Jug was a messy eater and he required regular cleaning, as did the floor area around his dish. In the time before he could eat and drink from a saucer, I had had to resort to wearing an apron to protect my clothes from his spillages, but lately I had detected a subtle change in his behaviour. He was becoming increasingly fastidious about his appearance. On one occasion, having washed him down with a wet sponge and dried him off as best I could with his towel, I happened to turn as I was leaving the room in time to witness another example of the little creature's instinctive efforts to become independent.

Silhouetted against a background of blazing logs, this miniature cat was slowly inching his way forward from the hand towel on which I'd left him. He moved purposefully across the stone hearth towards the inviting heat. On reaching the point he no doubt thought to be the warmest place on this earth, he stopped and, in complete repudiation of my recent efforts on his behalf, began to wash himself. This continued for a while until he slumped to a comfortable sleeping position and flopped on to his side in blissful abandon. Yet another hurdle in his development had been accomplished with aplomb. Thereafter, a considerable amount of his waking time was spent licking himself clean and tidy.

In the days that followed Toby Jug visibly improved in vitality and began to show a much more active interest in life.

I was much reassured by this, especially with regard to the latter, because a part of me wondered whether the problems he had suffered during those first weeks after birth might have damaged him. Now I could tell that these worries were unfounded and I became more aware of the bright and interesting character that was emerging. Toby Jug had proved himself very much the survivor *par excellence*.

Further aspects of his lively personality rapidly developed. For one thing, Toby soon began to show frustration at being kept in the jug – on several occasions he tried to climb out but his feline climbing skills just weren't up to scaling the smooth glass. He also became surprisingly mobile. Gone were the comatose slumbers of the early days. Whenever I let him out of his jug he would dart here and there in a sheer frenzy of leaps and bounds. Much to my astonishment, he played. I suppose it couldn't really be called playing by normal kitten standards but considering his size and what he'd been through, every mock pounce and roll were feats of Olympic proportions. A small ball of discarded paper became prey to be hunted down with exaggerated fervour. However, his energy very quickly ran out and he would quite suddenly drop in the middle of a half-completed whirl and fall immediately asleep where he lay.

At times, these antics left him lying asleep in the most undignified postures. Once I watched him playing outside his jug and jumping repeatedly at his reflection in the glass, probably through curiosity at what he thought was an apparition of another cat. Suddenly, he stopped, exhausted, lay flat on his back with all four paws in the air and, most comical of all, with just the tip of a pink tongue sticking out of his mouth. On such occasions I would pick him up and return him to the warmth and safety of his jug only for him to awaken some minutes later and begin shuffling around on the cotton wool, anxiously trying to catch my attention with piteous squeaks. On letting him out the same routine would start all over again and again until both of us were tired out.

In the evenings, having eaten, I liked to sit by the arched stone fireplace with only the flames from the fire and candlelight casting shadows that eased my mind in restful solitude. Now I had Toby Jug lying beside me as an extra comfort. Outside everything was still frozen in the harsh grip of the winter snows which made being inside the cottage feel extra cosy. At times like this I often left the curtains open to look at the moon through the bare branches of the oak and mountain ash trees that graced the far end of the garden. Whenever I sat like this, with the lights switched off and without any intrusions from the radio or television, I could sense a timeless affinity with the way of life many years ago which was much simpler than that demanded by our noisy, hectic and ultra-modern world. Despite my awareness that such a life was filled with hardships that I would never have to endure, I enjoyed indulging romantic thoughts about times past in Owl Cottage and of the people who lived here long ago.

Some people believe that houses have a spirit which epitomizes the feelings, good or bad, of the people who have lived there previously. Perhaps this is especially true of older houses because they have had a longer time to develop their spirits. Allegedly, houses built of stone are more likely to have acquired this characteristic because of peculiar qualities which enable stone to imbibe and store strong feelings. Whatever the truth of this, I noticed from the very first time I entered Owl Cottage that I experienced a sense of calm and friendly ambience. I had never felt anything like this in the modern flats and houses I had lived in.

The cottage always had a feel-good atmosphere about it. This feeling even extended to the garden. I could easily imagine a scenario in which hard-working ordinary family folk lived happily in this place and I felt certain the cottage retained something of their spirits. The sound of the wind in the trees, the calls of animals and birds and the crackling of the log fire seemed to link me to the people who had lived here previously. I found that these emotional vibrations, within both the cottage and the garden, had a calming effect on me, possibly because they derived from simple pleasures that had their source in nature rather than modern technology.

All of this may well have been my very own fantasy world and yet the singing of blackbirds as dusk settled over the garden or the night sky when the moon was at its fullest evoked emotions in me similar to hearing the Northern Sinfonia play Ravel at Brinkburn Abbey, or the sight of Bamburgh Castle clothed in a wintry landscape or sail boats in the harbour at Seahouses on a warm summer evening, as viewed from the balcony of the Olde Ship Inn. All of these things are part of the charm of Northumberland.

Toby Jug was the bonus I needed to cement my attachment to this Northumbrian world. Through observing his lust for life I was able to rediscover my lost youth and the hope of finding a place where I could experience a quality of living that fulfilled my wildest dreams.

In such a tranquil and philosophical state of mind, it was a bonus to have a cat on my lap to stroke even if that cat was intent upon tearing my best sweater to shreds. I enjoyed watching the emergence of such instinctive patterns of behaviour in Toby Jug as he became fitter, even though my sweater became increasingly tattered as he worked through the feline ritual of preparing a nest for sleeping. He presented a comical sight. Eyes half-closed in the sheer ecstasy of the war dance, with claws sharply extended, he treaded rhythmically to the tune of his own purring until eventually, turning a half circle, he collapsed. Then, with a few additional throaty purrs to convey his contentment, he fell asleep in an instant.

As he lay in my lap softly sleeping I could see that the bare patches of skin had responded to treatment and had just about healed. His fur now had a sheen to it, which was yet another sign of improved health, testimony to the good food he was getting and the days of intensive care, attention and love. To look at, he was nothing special compared to the chocolate-box pictures of kittens but to me he was the most remarkable kitten in the whole world. Beauty, as the saying goes, is in the eye of the beholder and to my eye Toby Jug was wonderful.

I remember at that time jotting down a few words that would aptly describe Toby Jug's appearance. He had a round knob of a head with tiny ears and almost the whole of his face was covered with untidy tufts of fur which gave him a wild, absurdly belligerent appearance. His face was covered with a predominantly black mask extending to below his nose where he had a white moustache slightly skewed to the right, along with a white mouth, throat and chest. He also had a black smudge on the right side of his nose which gave him a somewhat quizzical expression. The rest of his body was black except for neat white spats on all four paws that lent him an endearing touch of the dandy. His eyes, which turned green as he matured, were faintly ringed with white, giving him a perpetually startled look.

His appearance reminded me of some other creature that I couldn't at first put a name to until I recalled memories of racoons seen by torchlight as they raided re-fuse bins during the nights when I had stayed with friends in Rhode Island, USA. There was definitely a slight racoon-look to Toby Jug's eyes. When I stopped to think about it, there was a further resemblance to racoons in the way he would occasionally sit up and balance on his hind legs and look searchingly around. He also tended to scoop his food up into his mouth with a paw and sometimes he would dip a piece of cooked chicken I had given him into the water bowl before eating it. All of these behaviours were curiously racoon-like but at the time I didn't make a great deal of it. Later, however, it was to prove significant in consideration of Toby Jug's ancestry. He was certainly no ordinary cat either in looks or behaviour and in my opinion he was unique!

Taking a really careful look at him I wondered just how this little cat perceived the world and me. Maybe I was his entire world. I thought that any memory of his mother would be severely limited, especially since he hadn't been able to open his eyes until he'd been with me awhile. Be-cause I had been the first living and moving thing he'd ever seen, he probably regarded me as family and had im-printed in his brain the sight of me as mother. A famous zoologist called Konrad Lorenz once described how he be-came the 'mother' to some geese and had to teach them to swim and also how to fly by running along flapping his arms until the geese, imitating him, became airborne. Quite possibly, Toby Jug had no idea he was a cat at all but believed himself to be human. After all, he had never even seen another cat and had very little experience of associating with his own species. What else could he think in the circumstances, if he could think at all? It was all very confusing and I fell asleep in the chair ruminating on it.

Some hours later I awoke with a stiff neck to find that the fire was almost out and Toby Jug had worked his way up inside my sweater. Popping him into his jug, I blew out the candles and carried both kitten and jug up to my bedroom, which had an electric heater. I climbed into bed and fell nicely asleep, until Toby Jug's true cat nature began to assert itself once more and I awoke in alarm to find him squeaking and squealing. There he was, in the dim illumination of my bedside lamp, leaping urgently about in his jug, determined to attract my attention. Obviously, he wished to be let out of his jug to join me on the bed; 3 a.m. in the morning is no time to start an argument and so Toby won. Thereafter at bedtime he spurned his jug in favour of sleeping on the bed between the quilt and the top blanket as if it was his God-given right to do so. I expect his excuse would be that he had to keep track of me.

This was often the pattern of our evenings during the winter months as Toby grew from strength to strength and we became irrevocably attached to each other.

SPRING

With the coming of spring a whole new world opened up for Toby Jug and me in the northeast of England. In this part of the world, springtime brings more than just relief from winter, awakening the earth around us again in ways that more southern European climes enjoy for most of the year. The first greening of the trees and the bursts of vitality from crocuses, snowdrops and then daffodils in the gardens and woods are always welcome. I wanted Toby to enjoy to the full this first spring of his life. This particular springtime was especially anticipated because it would signify not only the passing of a severe winter but hopefully also mark the end of Toby Jug's life or death traumas. It was a time heralding hope that both he and I could take advantage of sunny days outdoors.

At first I didn't let him outside alone in the garden because I was afraid something might attack him. There were hawks and crows about, as well as weasels and foxes, and I was very much aware that Toby Jug wasn't big or strong enough to protect himself, nor was he at this stage sufficiently aware of danger or mobile enough to run away.

I had become accustomed to taking him almost everywhere I went in the cottage. Sometimes I just carried him in my hand or stuck him in the pocket of my wool cardigan with his head peeping out, so he could see what was happening. At other times I would place his jug near to where I was working, whether it was in the kitchen preparing food or at my desk in the study, so that he could keep me in sight. It was most important to him that he was able to see me wherever I was in the cottage – if he couldn't he would set up a rumpus which was out of all proportion to his size. His wails were no longer so feeble that they could not penetrate walls, even walls as thick as those in my cottage. Therefore, when I was at home I tried not to aggravate him by leaving him alone. It also made me feel guilty whenever he became distressed. I felt totally responsible for him and I liked to have him with me anyway.

He was not as yet physically robust enough to be given the freedom to run around the cottage on his own. There were lots of places that I was sure would attract the attention of the kitten when he was in his actively curious mode. There were cracks in the old skirting board and holes near the water pipes where spiders dwelt and where an unwary miniature kitten might disappear. It would take no end of ingenuity to retrieve him without demolishing part of the cottage. I consequently decided that until he achieved a decent size and weight I would restrict his access to certain parts of the cottage.

With the improvement in the weather now that spring was here I felt that it was warm enough to allow Toby to venture into the garden, but at first I judged it better for safety's sake to only take him out in his jug. The garden of the cottage was extensive and varied and for Toby Jug it promised to be a cat-wonderland of scents and sights. When he was capable of exploring the garden he would discover a multitude of natural delights which were the products of my time and effort.

When I first bought the cottage in 1964 it was much in need of renovation and the garden was grossly overgrown. Two years later, when Toby Jug came into my life, I had succeeded in clearing the lawn of weeds and the shrubbery had been cut back to manageable proportions. As I reworked each section I concentrated on planting roses and plum trees near to the house. The latter had a special significance for me. On a working visit to Hong Kong some years earlier I had been introduced to the ancient Chinese art of plum-tree painting, which dates back over a thousand years. In keeping with my interest in gardening I bought a famous book on the subject and discovered that plum trees flower with fragrant and fragile blossoms and the trees grow into extraordinary and aesthetically pleasing shapes which are quite unlike other fruit trees. According to Chinese folklore they are said to endow a garden with spiritual blessings for joy and health. I became so enthralled by what I had read about the beauty of these trees that I made up my mind to buy and plant some of them when I acquired a garden of my own. Now my plum trees, although still young, were beginning to assume what promised to be fascinating shapes and their blossoms, true to my expectations, were fragile flowers of sublime beauty.

In addition to plum trees I also planted a small orchard of apple, pear and cherry trees. I had also discovered a greengage tree in a local garden centre which I planted beside the plums. This veritable plethora of fruit trees meant that in early spring there was a display of blossom marvellous to behold. I also made a patio garden near to the back door of the cottage. Here I planted mulberry, blackthorn and some small crab-apple trees. In the centre of this small garden area I planted two dozen roses of various kinds selected for their perfume. This ensured that in both springtime and summer the garden adjacent to the cottage had plenty of colour and on a still evening the air was filled with sweet perfume.

Further into the garden I embarked upon an ambitious tree-planting project. Alder, white hawthorn, maple and old English oak were planted to border a winding gravel path leading up to the back fence where I had erected a summer-house. The spaces between the trees were given over to lawn and plantations of bulbs of all manner of spring and summer flowerings. Behind the stone-built double garage I dug a vegetable plot, which was bordered by a stone slab patio, complete with a masonry barbecue. Around the entire perimeter of the huge garden and drive I had painstakingly erected a

seven-foot wooden fence. My intention was to create a private garden paradise. I imagined that when Toby Jug was
eventually able to roam the garden he would have a whale of
a time. He was a lucky cat because all of this was his to share
and enjoy.

On evenings in late spring I loved to wander through the
garden of fruit trees in blossom simply to gaze at their delicate
flowers filled with coloured pollen dust and to feel at peace
with life and the universe. Listening to the calming sound of
their leaves as they stirred in the breeze was, for me, an insight
into the splendour of creation. As the evening became night I
liked to linger in the garden, especially when the sky was clear.

Later in the year, when Toby Jug was a mature cat, he
loved to share my night-time excursions and surprised me by
wanting to play games with me. He would disappear and
then suddenly reappear from out of the darkness, charging
at me, and then crouch in the grass before he reached me,
inviting a chase. When I made a mock dash towards him, he
would race away to leap up the garden fence and station
himself on the top in his lord-of-the-manor pose. It was interesting to see how his cat nature emerged so strongly at
nightfall. I was intrigued that he seemed to want me to play
with him as if I was also a cat. But this was still in the future
because for the present Toby Jug had a lot to learn about
the garden and about the feast of wonderful experiences it
had in store for him.

Whenever the weather permitted being outdoors at night, I was astounded at the countless stars I could see above me. The sight of this timeless universe always filled me with such wonder that it put my life and Toby Jug's into a very brief and insignificant perspective. At Owl Cottage, for the first time since childhood, I actually saw some shooting stars. The sight of them was a thrilling spectacle. I remembered to make a wish whenever I saw one.

Together Toby Jug and I could see all of this from the cottage garden, our window on the cosmos. To be here in this cottage garden and to experience all this was like a dream come true for the city boy who hated the enclosed boredom of school and played truant to wander through the woods and along the river banks (and was soundly beaten for it). Now I could indulge a keen delight in the freedom to enjoy nature as I wished. The prospect of sharing these wonders with Toby Jug gave my enjoyment of these simple pleasures a heightened perspective.

The daily happenings in the surroundings of the cottage had a prime quality about them which I stored in my mind. These included images of pipistrelle bats erupting from the eaves of the cottage and winging their dizzy flight-paths across the garden in the softening light of dusk. Or in the autumn twilight, a tawny owl calling from a nearby woodland copse whilst in the garden an adult female hedgehog, followed by two young ones, scoured the lawn, hunting for snails and slugs. I was always amazed at how rapidly hedgehogs could move.

When I bought the cottage I was intrigued by its name, Owl Cottage. It was only when I came to strip away the thick canopy of overgrown ivy and Virginia creeper that choked the stone walls at the back of the cottage that the reason became apparent. On the end walls of each of the three gables there were stone-sculptured owls of Victorian design. One of them was a fat brown owl of benevolent countenance, while the one on the highest gable was a tall thin owl with a look of the hunter. The third owl was the smallest of the three and bore the finely chiselled melancholic expression of the proverbial wise owl. I became very fond of this feature and made certain that the concrete around their bases was in a good state of repair to ensure that they would not be blown down in a storm.

All of this – the old stone cottage, the cottage garden with its trees, flowers and the shrubs – Toby Jug inherited in his role as the house cat. It was his garden as well as mine. Cats love a garden because it reminds them of their natural habitat: a place where they can pretend to be a wild animal again but with the option to lead a domestic life of civilized comfort when they wish.

I was fortunate to have a home where I felt at one with the wild Northumberland landscape. Owl Cottage amply fulfilled most of the conditions I had in mind when I was first searching for a rural property. Firstly, I had to be able to see trees from all of the windows and open doors. I have always loved to be near trees and to sense their living presence. In pagan times it was believed that each tree was governed by a spirit, something I don't find that hard to believe. When I'm gardening or sitting out in the garden, either in the early morning or late evening, I am always aware of each tree as a living presence. And as in the lyrics of the song from the musical *Paint Your Wagon*, I find it only natural that I should talk to them.

Another condition I had when I bought the property was that it had to be old and in this respect Owl Cottage suited admirably since it dated from the late eighteenth century. However, there must have been dwellings on the site before that because the road that passed outside the front of the cottage had been built over an aged horse-and-cart track linking the port of Amble to the many rural hamlets inland. There is a tale recounted from local folklore that Admiral Lord Horatio Nelson travelled on horseback along this track from his ship moored at Amble to meet up with his beloved Lady Hamilton at Linden Hall where she stayed as a guest of the Blackett family, who were important landed gentry. It is a romantic notion to think that the heroic admiral rode past my cottage door for his not-so-secret assignations. The local history of the area abounds in such tales, which serve to promote the aura of mystery that, traditionally, characterizes the Northumberland of bygone days.

One of the many selling points of the inside of Owl Cottage was the bathroom. It was an extension built out from the roof with a splendid wide-tiled windowsill spanning the whole width of the wall. Plenty of space here for toiletries and perhaps a houseplant or two, I thought when first viewing the property. Although I didn't know it at the time, plenty of space too for a certain cat to lounge in comfort. I also guessed that I would have a panoramic view of the sky when lying in the bathtub. But the best was yet to come. When I opened the window there was a breathtaking view of the Coquet Valley stretched out below. Over the tops of the huge trees, that would hide the river in summer, I was able to see far beyond to the hazy outline of the Cheviot Hills.

Further exploration of the cottage revealed a cramped attic bedroom which had an oval window facing east from which on a clear day I could just make out the blue outline of the North Sea about ten miles away. To my city-weary soul it was a sheer delight to consider the prospect of living in a place of such outstanding natural beauty. I set about buying it straightaway. When the deeds of the cottage arrived I was intrigued to read that it was forbidden to butcher a beast on the premises and that using the grounds for duelling would not be tolerated. Interestingly, though, I had noticed that some of the stones of the outside walls of the cottage were deeply scored as if they had been used to sharpen swords. Yet another romantic notion from the past!

Once it was mine, everything I discovered about the cottage enchanted me even though it required a lot of attention and much hard work and money to refurbish. Everything I did to improve it was a labour of love. The mysterious circumstance in which Toby Jug came into my life, I decided, was a good omen. It marked the end of the early years of professional striving and the solitude that usually goes with living in rented city flats. It also gave me a pet to care for and love. In return Toby Jug loved me with all the devotion of his being and filled an emotionally sterile gap in my life. An act of fate had brought us together and his struggle for survival helped me to evaluate what was of most importance in my own life.

The college where I worked was housed in a medieval castle owned by the Duke of Northumberland. The castle was situated in the town of Alnwick, often described as the Windsor of the North, whose feudal walls were surrounded by trees and fields that extended all the way to the farmsteads around my cottage. The quintessential rural landscape in which I found myself living was both a balm to my jaded spirit and a boost to my freshly awakened senses. It made for an improved and healthier quality of life. Even the air was sweet and full of the fresh aroma of flowers and woodland herbs. When the wind blew easterly the tang of the sea could be scented in the garden. Toby Jug's first experience of the outdoors reawakened me to the sights and scents of the natural surroundings as I witnessed his rapturous response to the garden.

When I first took Toby Jug out into the garden, I rested his jug on a flat stone on the wall fronting the rose garden and sat close by to watch his reactions. The effect upon him was beyond my expectation and showed something of the tough personality he possessed. Instead of cowering in the bottom of his jug, as I anticipated, he stood on his hind legs with forepaws pressed against the side of his jug and gaped at what was for him a whole new world. His small eyes bulged with excitement, his tiny head pivoted all around trying to encompass these new sights and his firm little tail wagged feverishly with the inevitable result that he suddenly fell and rolled over on his cotton-wool bed. Scrambling up on all fours he began to dash around his jug, frequently bumping his head in his eagerness to see everything. Finally realizing that I was at hand, he rushed to the side of the jug where he could catch my attention and whined piteously. He was obviously desperate to be let out. So despite my fears, I lifted him out of his jug and plonked him on the grass.

The experience momentarily paralysed him with excitement as he became aware of the smells of the garden at first hand. With eyes half-closed and nostrils quivering he looked to be in a state of pure ecstasy. Then, as he realized the immensity of space around and above him, his body began to tremble and shake all over. This situation lasted for several minutes before, at last, summoning up all his courage, he moved forward with exaggerated caution and deliberation. Moving only a few steps at a time and then halting to sniff the air, he proceeded as if he was stalking some huge and dangerous prey. After a while his movements ceased altogether and he lay down totally exhausted by his efforts. I guessed that the experience was proving too much for him. Tenderly scooping up the tired kitten, I laid him back in his jug whereupon he curled himself around as cats do and fell fast asleep. Toby Jug had made his first venture into the great wide world. He was no doubt now dreaming about his adventures, judging from the way his sleeping body gave occasional tremors, punctuated by squeaks, as if he was reliving the whole episode over and over again.

I decided to give him time to digest his encounter with the garden. There was a problem in that, for his own safety, I couldn't leave him out of his jug unless I could remain present. However, if I left him in the jug for security then he would not be able to see things clearly because of the distortion caused by the curvature of the glass and this would only increase his distress. Eventually, I remembered an old birdcage in the garage, left behind by the previous occupants of the cottage. I wondered if this might be the answer. With some difficulty I retrieved it from where it hung beneath a dusty beam. After cleaning it out I tried him inside. It seemed to solve the problem admirably, at least for the time-being. Far from objecting to this indignity, Toby Jug seemed very much at home in his cage and explored it with great curiosity.

The next day was sunny and mild so I thought I would try him in the cage on an upstairs window sill with the window open. From this position he was able to see the entire garden. He became very excited and agitated by the small songbirds whizzing between the trees. After a few days I felt confident that he could cope with the garden at first hand and with his usual affable approach to life he really began to enjoy the experience safe within the confines of the cage, which I moved around periodically on the patio so that he could have a different view of his world. This was also a secure way of familiarizing him with the garden in preparation for the time when he could wander at will.

Meanwhile, I was free to do some minor gardening jobs. As long as Toby could see me he was content but if he lost sight of me he would panic and cry out until we were reunited. Needless to say, on many occasions I got very little gardening done.

Fresh, sunny, spring days and chilly nights eventually gave way to mostly wet summer days and not so chilly nights. Toby Jug grew in size and gained in health. At long last I was able to dispense not only with his protective cage but also with the jug. It was clear that Toby would always be small in comparison with other cats but, considering what he was like when I rescued him, the change was gargantuan.

There remained, however, the problem of safety. How freely was I prepared to allow Toby to wander now that he had graduated from the protective environments of both the jug and the birdcage? I concluded that there would have to be limits imposed until he was mature enough to care for himself outdoors. The solution lay in buying him a harness.

One day I took Toby Jug with me to a local pet shop. The shopkeeper offered various harnesses for cats and rabbits which were far too large for Toby's small frame. The man, in his late sixties, was anxious to please and seemed both challenged and amused by the problem of getting a harness to fit Toby Jug. After desperately searching his mind, with a great deal of head-scratching, he recalled having specially adapted a fabric harness for his daughter's guinea pig which she had always insisted on taking with her when they went caravanning in the summer holidays. This sounded more hopeful. The only problem with this solution was that his daughter was now in her twenties and the guinea pig long gone. He was hopeful that she might have kept the harness for sentimental reasons because she had been inconsolable when her guinea pig had died and she was an inveterate hoarder. He promised to check with his wife and daughter that night and made a note to remind himself. I thanked him and promised to call the next day.

In fact, several days passed before I had time to call at the shop again although I wasn't really expecting anything to come of it. Meanwhile, Toby had to be confined to barracks. When I called again I took Toby Jug with me and the shopkeeper's eyes lit up when he saw us. He gleefully produced a small, brown, worn harness which he held aloft in triumph. It would be a perfect fit for the little cat he said, grinning from ear to ear, and so it proved. He was very pleased to have solved the problem and refused to accept any payment. I was delighted with the harness and Toby seemed very comfortable wearing it. Thanking him profusely I nonetheless bought a week's supply of cat food from the shopkeeper which I anticipated Toby Jug might eat someday when he grew out of his present addiction to canned baby food. I suppose I was spoiling him rotten but then I thought he deserved it and it pleased me to do so.

When I got home I again tried the harness on Toby Jug and it fitted perfectly, just as it had done in the shop, although Toby wasn't too sure about wearing it now that the novelty had worn off. Next, I measured out a length of twine which allowed Toby to range freely on his own. Attaching this to his harness and securing the other end to the leg of an iron garden chair, I set him free. He didn't move much at first and kept looking up at me to see what was required of him but eventually his attention was taken by some flying insects and he became engrossed. Now I could happily leave him for a while and get on with my jobs. This arrangement proved to be satisfactory as long as I remembered from time to time to change the place where I had tethered him.

For the most part Toby Jug was content to lie in the shade of a bush and watch the world of the garden go by, especially birds and butterflies. Occasionally, he would rouse himself to pounce on a fly which he then ate, quite a change from baby food. He seemed to appreciate the sights, sounds and the mysterious scents around him. I think it all unnerved him at times and he needed space to adapt. He always acted relieved when I untethered him and brought him back inside the cottage where he would start playing about more confidently in his familiar surroundings. Toby Jug was at heart a lap cat and at this stage content to be a house cat – a 'homebird' as the saying goes.

I recall one day buying some liquorice from the village shop and noting that Mrs Brown gave it to me in a white paper bag reminiscent of those used in the old-fashioned sweet shops of my schooldays. I was working at my desk and it so happened that just as I finished the last bit of liquorice Toby, who was then about twelve weeks old, was trying to clamber up my sweater. On a sudden impulse, more for amusement than anything else, I popped him into the sweet bag. Far from struggling to get out, he snuggled down and rested quite happily, with the paper bag wrapped around him and his diminutive, grizzled face peeping out of the top of the packet.

My enduring images of him at that early stage of his life are best described by words such as tiny, little, small, diminutive and so on. But for all that he had a strong body and a personality brimming with energy and curiosity as well as a huge capacity for affection. In addition, he had developed a deep-rooted attachment to me. To Toby Jug I was family and to me he was more than a cat. To me animals have unique personalities in the same way as people do. I have known budgerigars, cats, dogs and horses, each with their very own characteristics and personal ways of behaving which rendered them special, just like people. The cats in my life have all played an important part, helping me to understand the phenomena of animal behaviour and to realize that each of them is entitled to a life of their own. At a dinner party one evening I remember how I astonished a senior medical research scientist by asking him if he had ever considered, with regard to the cats and dogs he used in his vivisection experiments, that their lives were as important to them as his own life was to him.

My life with Toby Jug began to follow a routine that started at breakfast time, which he greeted with tremendous enthusiasm. It was the start of a new day and a fresh opportunity for him to savour life to the full. Apart from holidays and most weekends, breakfast tended to be a rushed affair because I usually needed to leave for work at about 7.30 a.m. Once we were downstairs Toby Jug insisted on being served immediately. He was always ravenous and I largely fed him on the best quality tinned cat food unless there were some roast beef or chicken leftovers from my meal the night before. Then, as he was eating, I would open the upper half of the back door so that he could answer the call of nature whilst I washed, shaved and got myself ready. After which, weather permitting, I would join Toby in the garden.

Mug of tea in hand we would gravitate towards the top end of the lawn. The view over fields and woodland towards the distant Cheviot Hills was balm to my mind before the demands of work. Toby, like most cats, was a fastidious washer and the morning ritual involved him vigorously licking and preening himself as he sat at my feet – it was a definite policy of his to be as close as possible to me whenever opportunity afforded – whilst I drank my tea and gazed at the view. Soon I would have to leave him and I would catch a glimpse of him in my rear-view mirror as I drove off, watching my departure from his vantage point at the top of the old apple tree by the gates. I hated leaving him and I knew that he missed me enormously but I could not take him into college and so he had to amuse himself all day until I arrived home in the evening, when he would be waiting with the warmest welcome a man could wish for. During the day when I was at work I always left one of the shed doors ajar so that he could make himself comfortable inside where there was an old clothes basket with a blanket inside and a dish of fresh water.

Breakfast on Saturday mornings was the best of the week. There were grilled venison sausages and lambs' kidneys bought from a country butcher in Rothbury and free-range eggs from a local man who boasted 'Fresh Eggs From Happy Hens'. I would also have wild mushrooms, when they were available, that I collected, accompanied by Toby, from the fields by the river where the cattle grazed and, from the nearby farm, slices of home-cured bacon dripping with flavour. Toby Jug would share some of the morning banquet with me, including some sausage and fried egg which I cut up for him, but not the bacon which he preferred to deal with by himself. When he had finished, he would lick his plate clean, jump down from the table, have a drink from his water bowl then go and wash himself in front of the fire, after which he catnapped until I called him to go out.

He loved sitting in the car whilst I drove around the town collecting the shopping for the week ahead. If, for some good reason I had to leave home without him on a Saturday, he would be inconsolable and truly 'miffed' with me when

I returned. This was because I belonged to him on Saturdays and he would do all in his power to insist on this priority. I must say that on the few occasions that I had to leave him I missed him too since I liked to think that the weekend was a time when both of us would enjoy being together.

Whenever I was able I would take him with me in the car on weekdays when my work entailed visiting schools to supervise students or when I was delivering cheques to landladies where students were billeted on special practice. On these occasions I would prepare a picnic for us to share and we had some memorable times picnicking in wild and picturesque rural settings of the Scottish Border towns from Duns to Lauder to Selkirk and beyond.

On one occasion I had parked alongside a row of old trees by a river bank. The car door was open for us to breathe the sweet clean air. Toby set off on a little prowl around. Generally, I still kept Toby on a lead when we went out on our jaunts, but I thought that he wouldn't venture far. Suddenly I heard sounds of a skirmish and spied a red squirrel's bushy tail in full flight, with Toby Jug in hot pursuit. The squirrel raced up a tall Scots pine and from a high branch set about scolding not only Toby but me as well. I retrieved my cat, just as he was contemplating a climb up the tree when I got the distinct impression that, far from having murderous intentions, he simply wanted to play as cats do when they chase each other backwards and forwards. However, I doubt whether the squirrel shared this view as it remained safely in the treetops until we resumed our journey.

Toby Jug's naivety was quite ingenuous. I thought that eventually he would mature into a killer cat, although yet again I had my doubts; he had probably become imprinted with too many human sentiments from living so closely with me and not having contact with his mother long enough to learn cat ways and cat lore.

On one warm spring morning in late May, Toby Jug and I were walking along a hillside path near the rural hamlet of Kirknewton when I stopped to gaze at some horses grazing in the valley below. After a while we continued with our walk. Toby Jug suddenly started pulling hard on his lead. In fact, he pulled so hard that he hurt his throat and we had to stop whilst he endured a fit of coughing. Looking around I saw what had excited his attention. Further along the path there was a grassy green meadow and it was full of rabbits feeding. 'Well,' I thought to myself, 'let him have some fun. He'll soon find out how fast rabbits can run.'

I slipped his head loose and off he went in a rapid stalking stealthy crawl with much tail swishing and wriggling of his behind. Of course, the rabbits had already spotted him and they fled to their respective burrows long before he got anywhere near them. However, it was then that I realized the mistake I'd made in letting him go because, far from giving up the chase, Toby Jug kept on going and disappeared down one of the rabbit holes. I raced over to the spot where he'd vanished and, crouching down as low as I could get to the rabbit hole, I began urgently calling him. To no avail.

Nothing stirred inside the burrow as far as I could tell and I was beginning to feel increasingly alarmed. What if the rabbits ganged up on him? Rabbits could kick and bite, as I knew from experience as a child who had kept one. I wasn't aware of just how long I spent with my face pressed to that sandy tunnel desperately calling his name when I suddenly became aware of voices above and behind me. I must have presented a strange if not ridiculous sight: a grown man with his head down a rabbit burrow, shouting 'Toby Jug!' Easing myself back to my knees I turned around with what must have been a shame-faced grimace and started lamely to explain what had happened when I stopped in jaw-dropping amazement. What I saw was a man standing staring down at me with a wide smirk on his face but what really astonished me was the sight of a second person. She was bending down stroking and talking to none other than his highness Toby Jug. I staggered to my feet and realized that Toby had obviously come out of another burrow entrance and had been watching me behind my back. He would have been puzzled at the sight of me lying fully stretched out with my head jammed up against the rabbit hole shouting his name. Both the man and the woman laughed heartily when I told them what had happened and continued on their way. Meanwhile I clipped Toby Jug's lead back on and decided that we'd had enough adventure for one day. We returned to the car and drove home with the Toby perched on my shoulder, purring loudly in my ear. Too late, I realized that I was wearing my brand new Harris tweed jacket.

Later that evening, after we had dined, I retired to the conservatory and was soon joined by Toby. I stroked and fondled him even though he had given me such a traumatic time during the afternoon. As far as he was concerned he had merely been having a jolly frolic. Nothing wrong with that was there? And it was then that I recalled my distress at several 'fun' incidents which had almost killed him in the past months. Banishing such thoughts from my mind as inappropriate in this restful setting, I was helped by the glowing sight of the planet Venus rising resplendent above the treetops, a golden star against the inky-black night sky. I took this to be a good omen for the future. Toby Jug was by now fast asleep and emitting faint snores. As I listened to him I wondered what new excitement this exceptional little cat would bring into my life. Tomorrow would no doubt herald yet more surprises.

I think that animals tend to be much more accepting of human beings than the other way around. I often found that cats took the initiative in my relationships with them. But it was a two-way process of communication. Whilst I sought to domesticate my cats, they made me more aware of the natural world by sharing their instincts and demonstrating their skills to me. And how fascinating they were. I totally reject the idea of the 'dumb animal' because I have never found it applied to any of the animals I have kept as pets. I've always found my pet cats to be graced by an in-born wisdom which perhaps many civilized human beings have lost. This was especially so with Toby Jug.

Toby Jug was, in a lot of ways, different from the many other cats I have known. He was more like a child to me because, in a sense, I had reared him and he knew no parent but me. I'm sure that some people would dismiss my feelings about Toby Jug as mawkish rubbish but I am equally certain that other people would echo the same sentiments about their own pets in spite of accusations of mad 'anthropomorphism' – the name given to attributing human behaviour to animals. Whilst all the animals I have known were special to me, Toby Jug assumed a significance in my life which was out of all proportion to the fact that he was a cat.

I don't think there is any doubt that, for many people, love, the strongest emotion of all, enters the equation when an animal becomes a pet. Sceptics would argue, though, that this love is only one-sided – without regular feeding, all of an animal's so-called affection would soon cease. I'm not so sure that this is true. In my experience animals need to be loved as well as fed, just as people do. I have known cats, dogs and horses who wanted to be stroked and petted, quite apart from their need for food. This was most certainly the case with Toby Jug who showed feelings of loving attachment for me beyond anything that I had experienced before with any other pet animal and it warmed my heart to feel it.

During my childhood there were always cats about the house, sitting on walls in the backstreets and in the gardens of the neighbours' houses and the backyards near my home. I recall the amusement when a cat got into our classroom at the local elementary school and how I was the one who managed to catch it and set it free outside again. I remember, too, the time that my grandmother's cat had two black kittens and my outrage and horror when my father drowned them in a pail of water because nobody wanted them and we were too poor to keep them ourselves. Most striking of all are my memories of my first visit to the zoo where I had to be dragged away from the tigers' compound. My wonder at those huge, beautifully marked cats knew no bounds. In my spare time I loved to read stories and look at pictures of the jungle cats of Africa and India. The favourite story of my boyhood was Rudyard Kipling's *Jungle Book* in which the Tiger, Shere Kahn, was my hero.

I also remember a striped tabby we had during the Second World War, when my father was away at sea. I found him as an abandoned kitten wandering the streets totally lost. My mother, with a family of three children to feed and only a pittance from the Admiralty to live on, reluctantly allowed me to keep it. I called the kitten Tiger. He was silver-grey with vivid dark stripes and he ate anything that was left-over from the family meals. He especially loved porridge. Tiger was always the first to run into the Anderson Air Raid Shelter with the family when the warning siren sounded to alert us to the German bombers which were mounting a blitz against the armament factories and the shipyards along the River Tyne. He survived the war but sadly was later run over by a lorry.

I have an almost instinctive attraction to cats. Whenever I see one I have to go and speak to it. For the most part cats come towards me and allow me to stroke them. I love to watch the graceful way that they move. To me, the most attractive dancers and actors have the skill of moving like a cat, that flowing smoothness which is a joy to watch. Teachers of yoga advise members of their classes to learn to stretch like a cat and to practise breathing exercises by moving the stomach muscles rather than the chest in just the same way cats do when they are totally relaxed. When I first saw Sean Connery as Special Agent 007 in the James Bond films I was captivated, as were audiences worldwide, by the speed and grace with which he moved; he walked with the stealth of a big cat.

It was because of these feelings that I was prepared on a cold winter's night to venture out in a snowstorm to rescue an injured cat. The reward for all my efforts was more than I could ever have expected. It was the bonus of turning a tragedy into a triumph: I found a dying kitten who grew into a wonderful pet called Toby Jug.

SUMMER

Summer was judged to have begun at Owl Cottage when the house martins arrived and diligently began to build their nests of dried mud and grasses against the stone walls high up under the overhanging roof of the cottage. It is fascinating to see the dark brown nests finally assume their full rugby ball shape with only the smallest of openings at the side for the birds to enter. Toby Jug sat on the lawn watching for hours, mesmerized by the comings and goings of these amazing birds. To me they were always a welcome sight in spite of the proliferation of their droppings which, as the season progressed, lay encrusted on the bedroom window-sill and marred the elegance of my much-prized and newly tiled patio.

During that first summer with Toby Jug there were many developments in the life we shared that surpassed anything I had encountered before with cats. For one thing he delighted in being with me, not for him the often haughty disdain that some cats show to their owners as an assertion of their independence. Whenever I called to him, he would come running to me from wherever he was, no matter what he was doing. This attachment extended even to travelling in the car. My work at the rural-based college entailed a great deal of travelling around the country visiting schools and other institutions and whenever possible I took Toby with me. He would sit or lie on the rear window shelf and slither enjoyably about as we took corners fast, much to the hilarity of passengers in other cars, especially children who often mistook him at first sight for a toy. On other occasions he would sit perched on my shoulder and purr into my ear at the sheer excitement of us travelling together. He never needed an invitation nor did he show any fear of travelling in the car. He was never car sick.

Wherever I took him he was always so exuberant that I was afraid of his recklessness. He would jump out of the car after me with complete disregard for traffic, big dogs or people who didn't like cats. With this problem in mind I resolved that he would have to be restrained in the same way as I had done earlier during his first ventures into the garden. However, the small guinea-pig harness I had acquired for him was too small now that he had grown and dog harnesses were too large.

One day I was browsing around in a pet warehouse store which had just opened in the city shopping mall. There I discovered a harness and lead suitable for a breed of small Mexican dog, the Chihuahua. These tiny dogs were a very popular choice of pets at the time. The harness seemed to fit the bill exactly and without further ado I bought it and eventually coaxed Toby Jug into wearing it. It was made of stiff new leather, unlike his other one which had been made of soft fabric. This one came around his chest and extended over his back so that if it was tugged it would restrain without choking him. He definitely wasn't very happy about wearing it but, being the valiant little fellow that he was, he accepted it. When I began to use it regularly he soon learned not to pull away. After a short while he got the knack and would run alongside me like a small dog. Occasionally, I would have to pull on the lead to guide him along and prevent him sidetracking but he gradually developed an awareness of what was required to keep in step with me and the arrangement worked out fine. I doubt if many cats would have accommodated so well to this restriction but Toby Jug was a fast and willing learner.

Using the harness, we were able to visit many places where few cats could ever have ventured. If danger threatened in the form of a large dog I would swing him up into my arms and, if necessary, fend off the attacker with the stick I carried on our walks. I can only remember a couple of such incidents happening. The vast majority of the time we had highly enjoyable, event-free excursions. For example, I had to supervise a student teacher on teaching practice in a school on Holy Island and, because I could keep him under control, I thought it would be nice to take Toby Jug along with me. Whilst having a cup of tea with the head teacher of the school I kept going to the window of her study to check that Toby Jug, whom I'd left in the car with the window slightly open, was all right. On our car trips, Toby would more often than not curl up and sleep away the time when I had to be involved in work matters, but occasionally he would become anxious as he used to be in the cottage during the first few weeks of life and then he would prowl around the car whining for me.

As I kept frequently getting up and looking out of the window, the head teacher became curious and, on learning the reason for my behaviour, she persuaded me to tell her the full story of the way I had rescued Toby Jug. She then told me she was a devoted cat owner herself and insisted on my bringing Toby Jug in to meet her. With some trepidation I agreed – what else could I do in the circumstances? And so I duly brought in Toby Jug and introduced him to the head. To my surprise he took to her immediately and purred loudly when she stroked him. I had, of course, been worried about his reactions to a stranger but he was fine and I was proud of him. Nevertheless, I thought the artful little beggar knows when he's well off as I watched him scoffing a saucer full of cream from the school canteen. The good lady had insisted on giving it to him as she said he must be thirsty after his car trip.

The head teacher was so taken with Toby that she prevailed upon me to allow her to carry him around the school to show the children. With a careful glance or two in my direction to reassure himself that I was following, Toby Jug, exhibitionist that he was, basked in the attention he attracted in the classrooms he visited. Never again would I need to worry about my little cat's capacity to adapt to other people. He enjoyed the whole experience hugely and responded beautifully, like a real star, to the children's affectionate curiosity. Before leaving the school the head told me that she intended to use the story of Toby Jug's rescue at the school assembly next morning to help the children appreciate how special animals are and how we need to care for them. It was a rare and happy experience for all concerned, especially Toby Jug, and it served to remind me that there are many other people in this world who love cats and share my feelings about them.

After I had completed my work at the school, as a special treat I took Toby Jug along the beach and bought us both a fish from a travelling fish-and-chip van which was parked in the lee of the castle near the bay. Toby Jug, sensible cat, ate only the juicy white cod flesh and not the batter, which I had to remove for him. After we had finished eating, and because it was such a warm sunny day, I let him off the lead to relieve himself and nose around while I kept a sharp lookout for stray dogs. Toby sniffed and roamed about where I was sitting on the beach. He apparently found the seaside smells quite delicious and investigated thoroughly a number of seaweed clumps that lay about the sand. He probably found it a welcome change to nosing around in his garden, but he didn't go far away. I don't think it would ever have entered his head to leave my side or to lose sight of me, not even for a delectable and most tempting scent. We both enjoyed our time out on the island. It was another perfect day.

While Toby Jug and I ventured far afield on my professional travels, it was at home that we spent most of our time together. He would always be at my side in the garden and often accompany me on short walks by the river bank and in the woods. During that first year of his life the things that I saw as just ordinary experiences of country life were for him new adventures, which were sometimes overwhelming and rather scary.

I can recall several such incidents which give a flavour of Toby's early life outside. For instance, on one hot summer's afternoon of sunshine, Toby was foraging in the long grass near where I was weeding a garden border. Suddenly, a sparrowhawk flew in low over the beech hedge and zoomed across the lawn on a flight-path that took it directly towards Toby Jug, who was hunting grasshoppers. In the instant that Toby Jug raised his head and saw the hawk coming straight for him he fled as fast as his legs could carry him to my side, jumped on my shoulder and conveyed his terror by biting the lobe of my ear. The result was that we both ended up in a state of shock whilst the sparrowhawk blithely went on its way, hedgehopping as it hunted for small birds and not the least bit interested in Toby Jug or the shock that I had suffered. For the rest of the day, when outside, Toby Jug was on constant alert and inordinately watchful of the airspace above him. Whenever and wherever I moved that day, he shadowed me closely.

On another occasion we were together in the garden enjoying the fresh air on what could be poetically described as a 'beauteous evening'. It was one of those delightfully calm summer evenings that are such a welcome change from our normal breezy and bracing climate in this part of the world. I was savouring the tranquil stillness of the trees and the scents from the flower beds whilst sipping a glass of claret. I noticed that Toby had climbed into the higher branches of the crab-apple tree and was busily investigating the insect-buzzing and small bird-fluttering among the leaves of the topmost branches. I gazed with pleasure at the sky as it became suffused with the delicate shades of colour that the Scottish describe as gloaming. Gradually, the sunset gave way to twilight and twilight was the time when the pipistrelle bats emerged from the eaves of the cottage to begin their insect-hunting aerobatics. The apple tree in which Toby Jug was perched was full of insects and when the bats came out they immediately began a strafing attack that Toby mistakenly believed was directed solely at him.

Cats are normally good climbers when going up trees but, like children, often find coming down a slower process of reversing and clinging on to the branches whilst at the same time glancing from time to time apprehensively over their shoulders. At least, that was the way Toby usually, and rather cautiously, descended from a tree-climbing expedition. Now though, with a squadron of bats hurtling around him, he reverted to what best can be described as 'flying squirrel tactics'. In alarmed desperation, Toby launched himself into a series of acrobatic swings from one branch to another that brought him perilously close to falling but also brought him swiftly to earth. Whereupon he headed straight for me and repeated his standing jump to my shoulder, his head whirling from side to side in fearful anticipation of an imminent attack from the skies. This time, thankfully, he didn't bite my ear but he did cause me to spill some of my wine. The bats continued their evening aerial display unperturbed as Toby refused to leave my shoulder until we were safely indoors.

This action of jumping on to my shoulder whenever something scared him soon became established as a habitual response to many other situations such as greeting me when I'd not seen him for a while, when he just felt particularly affectionate or when he wanted me to carry him. On reflection it was an athletic feat of gold-medal proportions for such a little cat and quite extraordinarily his own invention since no other cat of mine before had ever behaved in such a way. It could be quite disconcerting though when he didn't get his take-off just right and landed short of his target. Then he would have to crawl his way up over my jacket or sweater, which did my clothes no good at all! This behaviour worried me a little because Toby was an exuberant socializer. He loved company and would move from person to person for strokes and compliments and I feared that one day he might jump on some unsuspecting guest's shoulder and terrify them. But my fears proved to be unfounded. He reserved his shoulder leaps solely for me.

As Toby grew stronger I began to take him with me whenever I took short walks in the evening, especially now that he had his new harness. Usually, we followed the path through the fields that bordered a wide subsidiary stream of the River Coquet. Because a large expanse of the river bank had been fenced off to preserve private fishing rights, it was normally free from dogs and had become a favourite walk of ours. If Toby did see a dog coming he would run and jump on my shoulder even before I could haul him up by his harness. As usual on our walks, I had my stick ready to fend off any persistent barkers. They were few and far between.

Late one summer evening everything on our walk looked strangely different, perhaps due to it having been an exceptionally hot day. Ghostly white veils were rising from the damp fields and they skirted the trees and the holly hedges in swirling wreaths. Toby Jug, as was customary on our walks, was impatient to be ahead of me and since it was quite late and there was no one about, I unfastened his lead so that he could do some independent roaming. I often couldn't see him due to the ground mist which at times came up to my knees but I knew from experience that he would not stray far from my side so I wasn't unduly concerned. We had just passed the remains of an ancient ruin called Black Friars Mill when Toby Jug made a flying leap from the fog-covered ground to land, scrambling for balance, on a crumbling stone wall. He crouched there on full alert with his body straining forwards like a pointer dog as he stared into the mist. In the half-light he looked like a diminutive Black Friar ghost returned to haunt the place! From his appearance it was obvious that something had startled him. I followed the direction of his rigid gaze and there, emerging from the gloom like phantoms, were three dark forms which proved to be nothing more frightening than a vixen hurried along by her two romping cubs. I kept very still and the trio passed within three feet of us. A wondrous sight to behold but Toby Jug was not impressed. Casting a rueful glance in my direction he gave his back a quick wash just to show that he hadn't really been scared, and then we carried on with our spooky walk.

By late summer, when Toby Jug was about six months old, I felt reassured that he was here to stay and would not

There came a sszzzzing down the chimney as another bee dropped.

We remained for long moments captivated by the sunset.

We prepared to leave camp watched by many unseen eyes.

We sat in the moonlight by the weir, watching the salmon below.

suddenly be smitten by some terminal condition caused by his hazardous start in life. However, I was still not free from parental anxiety. I was uneasy about the possibility that he might catch cat flu or pick up something lethal through contact with another cat. Then there was the worry that, as he matured into a full-grown tom cat, he would go off seeking to mate with female cats. I had heard stories of male cats disappearing for weeks on end in search of a female cat on heat. All of these potential problems had but one solution and that was a visit to the vet.

If Toby was concerned at all by traumatic memories of the tragic loss of his mother and brother and his own near demise on his introductory visit to Mackenzie the Vet, he didn't show it. I took him into the clinic and sat him on the same wooden table from which I'd snatched him away that terrible winter's night not a year ago, literally from the jaws of death.

'So you succeeded in rearing the wee thing,' Mac exclaimed, all smiles as he recounted the tale to his young female assistant. 'Well he seems strong enough for us to neuter him now,' he said amiably, as Toby began to display the first signs of alarm at the feel of Mac's rough, searching hands.

'I'll give him his injections too. Aye, he's turned into a bonny wee thing all right; all power to you,' he grudgingly conceded as he whisked Toby away. 'You can call back for him in a couple of hours' time, aye?'

Suddenly I was alone, not knowing what to do with myself. Would Toby Jug die under the anaesthetic? Why hadn't I left him intact to enjoy his life instead of putting him through this? These were the questions that kept coming and going through my mind while I waited, fearful of the awful things that might happen to him.

I spent almost two hours in a tea shop in Alnwick agonizing about it all. After two hours and one minute I was back at the vet's surgery. Mac was there examining a huge but gentle Labrador as I entered the surgery area. After a moment he glanced my way and to my immense relief said, 'You'll be wanting your wee cat now.'

With that remark he disappeared. He clearly hadn't heard my hoarsely voiced question, 'Is he all right?'

Shortly afterwards, Mac returned with Toby Jug, looking slightly flustered and pained by what had happened to him but none the worse for all that. Toby celebrated our reunion with his habitual fulsomeness and ended up in his usual position on my left shoulder. I revelled in this public display of our bonding and indulged happily in the look of astonishment on Mac's face. I took the vaccination and other certificates he handed me and headed out to my car with Toby Jug clinging on to my shoulder like a koala bear.

Happily reunited we headed homewards with me whistling happily and Toby Jug still perched on my shoulder as we drove along. His claws dug in as he hung on over every bump in the road but I didn't mind a bit. I was so happy to have him back with me, alive and well. Before we left the vet's surgery Mac's young assistant had handed me a tablet which, she explained, contained an antibiotic to prevent any infection after Toby Jug's operation. I told her that Toby would not take a tablet of any kind and that I had tried unsuccessfully on several occasions to administer some proprietary health tablets for cats.

'Oh nonsense,' she exclaimed. 'Look I'll show you how to do it.' And with that remark she took hold of Toby Jug's head and to his astonishment quickly prised open his mouth and popped the tablet in. 'There you see, as easy as that,' she said. Toby snapped his mouth shut and stared pop-eyed at me in amazement.

After we had been on the road for quite some time, I heard a 'Pitttth' sound from Toby. What remained of the said tablet was spat out and landed in my lap. He had kept the offending tablet in his mouth and waited until he was well away before spitting it out. So much for the expertise of callow young vets. I chuckled as Toby Jug, obviously feeling pleased with himself, purred loudly in my ear all the way home.

On arriving home Toby seemed to be suffering no ill-effects after his operation and ate a specially prepared meal of chicken livers with his usual gusto. However, when I went to file the veterinary certificates I noticed something strange. Under the column headed 'Breed of Animal' there was written in bold handwriting: 'Cat: Black & White Long Haired Maine Coon'. I looked down at Toby Jug happily eating away and thought, 'What on earth is a Maine Coon?'

I looked at him with new eyes. Here I was thinking of him in the most affectionate terms as an ordinary 'moggie', but perhaps he was really a special breed of cat or some kind of hybrid. More than slightly bemused, I resolved to try to sort out Toby Jug's past history as soon as possible. The thought of telephoning Mac to ask him for information did cross my mind but I neither wanted to appear ignorant nor did I want to give him any satisfaction if he was playing some kind of joke on me. The local library in Alnwick couldn't help me at all but then on an impulse I telephoned the area RSPCA and a kindly woman's voice informed me that a Maine Coon was an American breed but apart from that she couldn't tell me any more. All the more intrigued, I determined to pursue the matter further. For the next five days I was going to be in Oxford to speak at a conference so I thought that I would take some time out to do more research there about the Maine Coon breed.

Assuring him that I would soon return, I left Toby Jug in the loving care of my mother and set off for Oxford on one of my rare trips away. It was the first time Toby and I had been separated overnight. A short distance from St Catherine's College, where I was staying, I discovered what I was searching for in Blackwell's bookshop at William Baker

House on Broad Street. There, in the Natural History Section, I found, among the various cat books and reference authorities, a photograph of a cat almost identical to Toby Jug. It was described as a 'Black and White Maine Coon'. So Mac was right he hadn't been kidding me.

Scanning the information which followed I found a very comprehensive description of semi-long-haired breeds of cat starting with the Maine Coon. There before me lay the full historical details of my little cat's ancestry and an interesting one it was, too. It appeared that the Maine Coon was so called because the breed originated in the American state of Maine. The explanation of the name Coon was that it derived from a mistaken belief by the inhabitants of Maine who thought that, because of the cat's similarity in looks and mannerisms, the animal was the result of crossbreeding between cats and racoons. According to scientific evidence, this is not genetically possible.

As I read on it became clear that cats, such as the Norwegian Forest cat and the Persian Longhair, were taken on board sailing ships to kill rats and as a result they were introduced to North America by seafarers from Europe. The ship cats most likely interbred with the local short-haired cats to eventually produce, by a process of natural selection, the Maine Coon. This breed became very popular and appeared at cat shows in the USA as early as 1895. I was fascinated by all of this and it made me ponder just how a breed of cat from over 3,000 miles away in the United States could have turned up in a semi-wild cat's litter just over a mile-and-a-half from my cottage in Northumberland. But then I suppose sea traffic goes both ways and cats are inveterate and promiscuous breeders. Whatever his background might be, it was clear that Toby Jug was an identifiable living descendant of the American Maine Coon breed.

I was further intrigued when I read the description of the particular temperament associated with the Maine Coon breed. The picture the book portrayed was a 'spitting image' profile of my Toby Jug. I read that Maine Coon cats are friendly, good-humoured and uncomplicated cats that are highly adaptable. They are inquisitive and tend to retain a kittenish attitude to life even when fully grown and mature but they are easily bored and therefore need constant variety and stimulation; they love to romp and play and become easily attached to people, more especially to one or two persons who are primarily involved in their care and upbringing. This, in a nutshell, was Toby Jug as I knew him.

Reflecting at leisure on what I'd learned, I recalled the night of the rescue and the appearance of Toby's mother. She had a long body with a lengthy, fluffed-out tail that was darker in colour than her body, which was a light silver-grey. I remembered thinking what a beautiful cat she must have been as I watched her on the vet's table that awful night.

Consulting again the *Encyclopaedia of Cats*, the book by Esther Verhoef which I'd bought that morning, I leafed through the photographs. On page 34 I saw once more the image of my Toby with the description 'Black and White Maine Coon'. As I flicked further through the pages I came at once upon the familiar face of the cat I had freed from the gin-trap and had last seen in her death throes. The simple inscription below the coloured photographic plate read 'Silver Black Tabby Maine Coon'. Toby Jug's mother, from my memory of her, had looked very similar. And so I thought if Toby Jug is really a descendant of the Maine Coon breed then it followed that either or both of his parents must have been Maine Coon. I resolved that on my return from Oxford I would make some local enquiries.

Back in Northumberland, I was delighted to be re-united with Toby Jug who ran and leapt on to my shoulder the moment he saw me. Obviously we had missed each other but it must have been worse for him because he wouldn't have been able to understand that I'd be coming back for him. He had been well cared for by my mother but, of necessity, he had been locked indoors in one of the old stables on her land for most of the day. This was a precaution we had worked out before I left to prevent him wandering off in search of me and his home. My mother said that he hadn't eaten much and seemed to be suffering from homesickness in spite of all the attention she had lavished on him. We were glad to be together again and we soon resumed our happy life at the cottage.

Whenever you want to know about anything in my village, there is always one sure place you can go. It's the place where people gather of an evening to relax over a drink and talk, namely the village public house. Felton has two pubs: the Northumberland Arms and the Stag's Head. Over the course of several nights and a weekend soliciting gossip in the two aforementioned hostelries, I discovered that there was a woman who bred pedigree cats in the nearby village of Shilbottle. In Shilbottle Post Office my attention was directed to a typed note amongst the advertisements with an address in the village where pedigree cats were for sale.

It didn't take me long to find the cottage which was set back from the road in an extensive garden. I walked up the well-kept drive that was bordered with a wide variety of flowering plants and shrubs. A Victorian-style wrought-iron gate led to an inner paved area and a huge front door. The cottage branched out on both sides of the frontage in keeping with the style of the period. The windows upstairs had old-fashioned wooden shutters which I noticed were closed even on this warm, sunny afternoon. It struck me as rather odd but then possibly there had been a bereavement or loss in the family which necessitated a time for mourning. I did not wish to intrude unnecessarily on private feelings but I was anxious to pursue my quest, so I rang the bell and waited in anticipation. A frail woman of mature age answered the door and, on hearing my inquiry, invited me inside. I introduced myself to her and learned that she was called Sarah Erskins, that she was a widow who lived with her daughter and that she was a specialist breeder of thoroughbred cats.

There were well-groomed cats everywhere in the sitting room into which I was shown. There were Persian Longhairs, Colourpoint and Sealpoint, Siamese, Abyssinian Reds and Balinese Bluepoints, all of which she identified by name for my benefit, but there were no Maine Coons as far as I could tell. Over a cup of tea, standard local hospitality, I asked her if she'd ever had any Maine Coon cats. Her expression became serious and pained at my question and instead of answering she rose and walked over to an old writing desk just like the one my grandmother had. Rummaging about in the draws she withdrew a photograph album. Quickly turning the pages she found what she wanted and placed the album on my knees.

There before me lay an enlarged photograph of a silver cream tabby female Maine Coon. Underneath was inscribed her name: Silver Girl Bonny and there was a certificate pasted on the same page which identified her as being registered with the Governing Council of the Cat Fancy (GCCF). I was both surprised and a little shocked to see that the cat pictured was one and the same she-cat I had rescued on that fateful January night. There could be no mistake. At the sight of her picture I was transported briefly back in time to the wind-swept and tumbledown hayloft where I had found her with her kittens. Suddenly the voice of Mrs Erskins cut through my reverie and I looked up to see tears in her eyes.

'She was my Bonny,' she said with feeling. 'And we lost her! And I haven't had the heart to seek a replacement for her. How could I?'

With that she sat slowly down on the edge of her armchair and I waited patiently for her to go on.

Holding her cup tightly in both hands, without drinking from it, she stared intently at the carpet as she recounted the story of her loss.

'We were taking her to the Harrogate show along with Bluebell and Chi-Chi. Bonny was such a pet, I used to let her sit on my lap during most of the drive. I wish now I'd kept her in the show cage with the other two cats,' she said tearfully and paused. I sipped my tea in silence until she was ready to go on.

'My daughter was driving and on the spur of the moment she decided to call at the Running Fox in Felton for a newspaper and some sweets for the long journey.'

I nodded to indicate that I knew where she meant.

'Having parked in front of the shop she opened the rear

door of the Land Rover to get her handbag. Then she came around to my side and opened the passenger door to ask what she could get for me. At that exact moment two RAF jets flew low-level over the village. The noise was like a thunderclap and both of us nearly jumped out of our skins. Then I realized that Bonny was gone. She must have been startled when the planes flew over and fled. We never saw her again,' she sobbed.

'We searched for hours but there was no sign of her. We never got to the show. In the evening both my son and daughter went looking for her as I was too upset to go. We have heard nothing since even though we've put notices around and offered a reward, nothing, nothing at all.'

Her voice tailed off as she sagged back in her chair in despair. Looking at the expression on her face I remembered what it was like to lose a pet cat and never know what had happened to it. Only in this case, I did know and felt duty bound to try to ease this poor woman's feelings but I hesitated in case I caused her even more grief.

I looked again at the photograph. I had to be sure now that the she-cat I'd rescued and the missing Bonny were the same before I said anything to her. Just then my dilemma was resolved because she looked straight across at me and said, 'You know something. Tell me,' as she leaned forward in her chair. 'Has she been found?'

I spared her the gruesome details as far as I could. But I saw just how shaken she was to hear of Bonny's death. For several minutes after I'd finished my account she remained silent, staring into the fire, then she said: 'You say there's a kitten? A hybrid?'

I nodded, fearful now of what she might want.

'Tell me about the kitten,' she said.

I told her briefly about Toby Jug, how he looked and how he was and lastly how much he meant to me. Her face positively beamed as she said, dabbing at her eyes, 'So there is a happy ending to this after all.' A noise from the hallway announced that her daughter was home from work and, leaving her to retell the tale, I left. She followed me to the door and, pressing her frail hand on my shoulder, she thanked me for what I'd done for Bonny and her surviving kitten.

I waved from the car as I drove away and reflected on the tremendous depth of feeling a pet animal can generate in a person's life and then I recalled reading somewhere that the RSPCA had estimated that there were at least five million cat owners in the UK. So many people have a great affection for cats. I knew what Mrs Erskins was feeling because I felt the same way about Toby Jug.

'Well,' I sighed to myself. 'Now I know who his mother was perhaps I can trace his father as well.'

This idea ranged through my mind until I arrived home. The thought kept coming back to me for days afterwards.

Eventually, I decided that at some time in the future I would have to investigate this whole matter further but then fate took a hand again.

I cannot honestly say that Toby showed any emotion at the news about his mother but merely yawned in that off-hand way that cats have when they are bored with the conversation. I expect to him it was dim dark history and in no way to be confused with the bliss of his current life. Nevertheless, I did tell him about her as a matter of duty and for her sake. Now that I knew more about Toby's background and inherited characteristics, I studied him with new eyes and decided that the two words I would add to the descriptions of a Maine Coon cat's personality would be 'mischievous' and 'perceptive'.

Toby Jug was remarkably brainy for a cat and sometimes quite deceptive with it. He was also quick to tune-in to what people were thinking, as I found out many times, including when I bought him a small red ball to play with whenever I had to leave him alone in the cottage. It was the kind that bounced easily and, if struck even moderately by a playful paw, would shoot across the room in a way that invited a headlong chase. Toby Jug loved this plaything and would sometimes carry it around in his mouth and occasionally bring it to me to be thrown so that he could jump and attempt to catch it. Here again was a link to his Maine Coon breeding since these cats are well-known for retrieving small objects and carrying playthings to their owners.

One day the red ball disappeared and couldn't be found. Obviously, Toby had carried it out of doors and it had gone astray somewhere in the garden. No amount of careful searching unearthed the lost ball. Tired of searching we eventually abandoned the hunt as a lost cause and I made a mental note to buy him another. Some days later I was puzzled to find a number of tomatoes lying around the patio, some of which were in a severely bruised state. When I set about retrieving these I noticed that Toby looked suspiciously guilty and I became quite perplexed at what was going on. Was Toby Jug bringing these tomatoes and if so where was he getting them? It was most bewildering.

The mystery was solved several days later when Alice, the neighbour from the cottage next to mine, knocked on my backdoor and told me, with some embarrassment, that she really liked my little cat but could I stop him from going into her greenhouse and stealing her tomatoes. She explained that she left the greenhouse door partially open for ventilation. Then it dawned on me what had been happening. I started to give her an account of the saga of Toby's lost little red ball when, to my horror the villain of the piece appeared around the corner of the cottage in full view of both of us, carrying a red tomato in his mouth.

I have always believed that animals, and more especially cats, have a full range of emotional sensitivities which includes a conscience. At the sight of the two of us, Toby Jug skidded to a stop, dropped the tomato and scampered off to hide in the bushes. I assured an indignant Alice that I would remonstrate with Toby Jug (although at the time I wasn't quite sure how I would do this) and punish him at the earliest opportunity. I also mentioned that I would buy Toby a multitude of small red balls that very afternoon. I suggested that for a few days she might like to close her greenhouse door. I communicated all of this in the most apologetic manner I could summon, stopping short only of getting down on my knees to say sorry. I did offer to buy her some tomatoes from the village shop but this only seemed to add insult to injury since she angrily assured me that her tomatoes were homegrown and far superior to any that were store bought. We parted on reasonably good terms, though, and I resolved to buy the dear lady a bunch of flowers and a box of chocolates as a peace offering. This I duly did and friendly diplomatic relations were re-established.

Thankfully nothing more was ever heard of the tomato incident, but I suspect that Alice took steps to prevent Toby's entry into her greenhouse. After his exposure as the tomato thief Toby was not seen until mid-evening, when hunger pangs overcame his guilty feelings. When he did at last appear for his dinner I confronted him with the stolen tomato and let him off with a light scolding and, from the shamed look he affected, I was sure he understood me only too well. The scolding appeared in no way to diminish his appetite, though, and merely served to confirm for me the inherent resilience of a cat's nature to shrug off adversity.

Following this incident I made sure that my other neighbours were aware of Toby Jug's eccentricities and, fearful of angry reprisals against him, I offered compensation for any damage he might in future cause. But in the small community in which we lived Toby Jug had quickly become accepted for the playful character that he was. His friendly, extraverted nature tended to ingratiate him with the neighbours, especially the ladies of the households, some of whom regularly saved titbits of cooked meat and fried bacon for him.

Since that event Toby was given a regular supply of red balls which periodically had to be changed, either because he forgot where he last played with his ball or because the old one had too many bits chewed out of it and he liked me to supply him with a new one. I often found discarded balls in unusual places, like in cupboards, under the bed, in the vegetable rack and once behind a cushion on the sofa, not to mention those discarded in the garden. This made me suspect that there was a conspiracy afoot – something of the order of T.S. Eliot's 'Macavity – The Mystery Cat' (described as 'the Napoleon of Crime!') – but I never could catch him at it, which led me to suspect him all the more. Toby Jug, I'm glad to say, was developing into quite a maverick personality.

There was, however, something which perturbed me about the incident recounted above which had nothing to do with tomatoes but everything to do with the way that cats, unlike any other domestic animal, wander as they please. I could not control Toby Jug's excursions unless I tethered or imprisoned him all the time, which was to my mind unthinkable, especially since we lived in such appealing surroundings. Also I hated the idea of caging any creature. Some pet owners who keep caged birds may care for them in such a way that they have a good life, but my own feelings for Toby Jug prohibited restricting his freedom to roam. With regard to the need to give Toby Jug the freedom to wander at will, I was anxious to know what rights cats had under the law.

I raised this point with a police inspector friend of mine whilst we were having a drink together one night in the Northumberland Arms. The gist of what he told me was that a domestic cat cannot be owned in law by anyone, it is not property as such nor is its owner obliged to be responsible for whatever it does on its wanderings. He also added, with respectful deference to my feelings for Toby Jug, that cats are classed in the same category as vermin such as rabbits, rats and mice. I trusted my friend's words and did not consult a solicitor on this point because it just seemed to be the way things were. Yet the prospect of Toby Jug's wayward adventures worried me considerably to the extent that I felt I must do something about it. I was also aware of scare stories about cats being abducted by unscrupulous people to be sold to laboratories for vivisection and other kinds of experiments.

Consequently, I bought Toby Jug a collar, a fine collar of fluorescent yellow plastic (so that I would more easily spot him in the darkness), with a bright silver bell attached. The collar had a strip of elastic built into its length as a safety precaution so that, in the event of it becoming hooked on to something, it would slip off the cat's head without harming him. Also, I bought a miniature brass cylinder containing a slip of paper with my name, address and telephone number and the words 'Reward for return of this cat'. I didn't put Toby's name on it in case someone stole him. But in this way I sought to protect Toby Jug as my cat by means of 'Common Law', since the collar and identity cylinder were certainly my property.

In the last few weeks of the summer term, whilst I was still very busy at the college, I had given Toby Jug the freedom to wander and play as he wished rather than shutting him in the house or tethering him on a lead in the garden. I believed that he was now mature and experienced enough to manage on his own, and he had his brand new collar. He loved the freedom and coped very well with his newfound independence. As far as I knew he stayed close to home and ventured over the fence to other gardens only where he was welcome, except of course for his clandestine visits to Alice's greenhouse. But as my homecoming time approached he would always be waiting in the drive to welcome me. Until this particular day.

When I returned home on a Friday afternoon I was confronted by the worst fear any pet owner can have. Toby Jug was nowhere to be found.

Generally, he would sprint to my side from wherever he was playing or reposing as soon as he heard the car approaching. If he was not there to greet me immediately I had only to call his name and whistle and he would come running. On this occasion I whistled and called his name many times, but to no avail. This was most unlike him and I began to panic. First I checked the roadway outside the cottage. Had he been run over and left lying at the roadside? Thankfully there was no sign of him there. But then I began to think of other equally dreadful alternatives. Had he got caught by his new collar and strangled himself? Many alarming thoughts and improbable scenarios filled my mind as I searched everywhere I could think of looking.

All the while I could feel myself becoming more and more panic-stricken. He had never done this before and I began to fear the worst. Something terrible must have happened to him. Sad memories of pet cats disappearing without trace flooded my mind. As I rushed here and there in a lather of anxiety, I was stopped in my tracks by a faint whine which seemed to come from above. Glancing up with relief, I spotted Toby Jug high on the conservatory roof that sloped up to my bedroom window. In the throes of panic I had failed to look for him on the roof.

He turned when I called his name and gave me another whine of recognition but then turned his attention back to the window. He began to make the strangely aggressive chittering sound with his teeth that he sometimes made when watching birds through the kitchen window. He made no attempt to come to me and was obviously engrossed in something or other within the bedroom. Puzzled by this odd behaviour, I decided to investigate the bedroom from inside the cottage; perhaps a bird had flown down the chimney and was fluttering around the room, causing Toby Jug's displeasure.

As I climbed the stairs I could hear a strange humming noise coming from behind the bedroom door. I flung the door open, only to slam it shut again instantly, aghast at what I had seen. The room had been invaded by a swarm of bees. My bedroom, as I briefly saw it, was black with their presence. They must have come down the chimney and in through the fireplace.

A neighbour, who had noticed the tail end of the swarm clustered around one of my highest chimney pots, kindly offered to summon the help of a friend who kept bees. I was confused and disturbed by this situation and in the circumstances any offer of help was to be welcomed. Meanwhile, I still couldn't entice Toby Jug down from his vantage point since he seemed obliged to stand guard by the window.

We waited, a little group of neighbours, looking skywards to check on the situation and I listened with a sinking heart to tales of doom about rogue swarms of bees that invaded houses and drove the occupants out, sometimes for days, sometimes for weeks, until a solution could be found. A murmur of expectancy arose from the small crowd as the friend of my neighbour arrived in his van. The curiosity of this peaceful community, normally starved of dire events such as this, was fully aroused and news had spread by word of mouth from one cottage to the next. Soon an appreciable number of onlookers had gathered to witness the excitement.

After introductions and a brief consultation with us, followed by a quick inspection of the cottage interior, the beekeeper thoughtfully appraised the situation. Then, undaunted by comments from the crowd such as, 'You wouldn't get me to go in there for a thousand pounds', he prepared to tackle the problem at first hand. Armed with various beekeeper's hoods and nets he marched upstairs, with a boldness and professional aplomb that was truly impressive, and entered my bedroom, closing the door firmly shut behind him. Before going into the cottage he had told us that his purpose was to locate the queen bee and bring her out and this would result in the swarm then dispersing. At least, that was the carefully worked-out plan. Toby Jug meanwhile, maintaining his vigilance on the conservatory roof, had by now moved up to peer into the window, his courage no doubt strengthened by the arrival of reinforcements. He still would not come down.

As the beekeeper disappeared inside the cottage a hush came over the crowd. We waited for several minutes in silent anticipation. Suddenly there came exclamations of pain and anger from inside the cottage, which caused cries of alarm from the waiting onlookers. Then, the beekeeper erupted from the back door of the cottage and hurtled into the yard. Several angry queen bee guards had seemingly penetrated his protective attire. He flung off his face-mask, uttering various unrepeatable expletives. For a while all was confusion as my neighbour and I tried vainly to help by swatting his clothing whenever another bee appeared or wherever we thought there might be one. Far from being well-received, this attention only seemed to add to his stress and exasperation. By now the bee expert was becoming increasingly distraught and had totally lost his calm and confident demeanour of a few minutes ago.

The crowd, anticipating an angry scene, began to drift away. Finally the beekeeper lost his temper completely and vented his spleen in no uncertain manner on my neighbour, myself, all species of bees and the universe in general. Having been severely stung and suffered the public indignity of defeat, he stormed out of the yard and roared off in his van, leaving behind only the stunned aftermath of his wrath and a few dead bees as evidence of his efforts. Deeply apologetic, my neighbour returned to the company of his television, shaking his head in commiseration and remarking that his friend had always been known to have a volatile disposition. All at once I found myself as alone with the problem as before except that now the bees were humming even more aggressively. Toby Jug and I had been abandoned to our fate.

Eventually I managed to coax Toby Jug down from the roof with the promise of food and we both warily entered the kitchen where Toby Jug gulped down his meat morsels all the while looking around apprehensively as he listened to the aggressive humming coming from upstairs. A simple little cat he might be, but he knew peril when he heard it. Having finished his meal in record time, he rushed outside, still licking his lips and burping with the haste of his eating. Having made his escape he sat on the kitchen windowsill anxiously awaiting further developments.

'Coward!' I accused him, but Toby Jug was unmoved.

Left to my own devices I pondered the situation and after a cup of tea I decided upon my own battle plan. I would light the fire downstairs and load it until it was a roaring inferno. Then, since it used the same chimney vent as the fireplace in my bedroom, the bees would be persuaded to go elsewhere. I stoked the sitting room fire into a furnace of heat and observed from outside with some satisfaction that the swarm around my chimney stack had grown considerably as they retreated out of the chimney away from the heat and smoke. But relief soon turned to dismay because, as the fire died down, the bees once more crowded back inside the chimney. It was a stalemate. To add to my distress Toby Jug refused to come into the cottage. No amount of coaxing could change his mind.

Back in the sitting room, I determined to keep the fire as hot as possible to prevent the bees from occupying the whole house. Obviously, I couldn't sleep upstairs. Instead, I was forced to use the settee as a makeshift bed. Nor could I use the bathroom, which contained all my toiletries, because it was en-suite to my bedroom. Fortunately there was a primitive outside toilet but I had only the kitchen sink in which to wash. It really was an uncalled-for nuisance and showed one of the downsides of country living. In a mood of abject misery, I wondered what I should do next.

Soon it began to grow dark and as I was very tired after the day's exertions I decided to turn in for the night and somehow find a way to deal with the problem the next morning. Before locking up I went outside and, to his alarm, grabbed Toby forcibly from his refuge on the windowsill and brought him into the cottage. Then I shut us both in the sitting room after first filling the coal-scuttle, not to mention the fire, to ensure maximum burn. We were in a state of siege. In case of a bee attack I armed myself with a rolled up newspaper and prepared to repel any invaders. I also jammed the gap between the floor and the bottom of the door with a blanket I took from the car to prevent any bees entering the room whilst we slept. Toby Jug, far from settling down, began to prowl around the room looking for a way out. Ignoring him, I lay down and tried to rest.

We spent an uncomfortable night, tossing and turning, and it was a relief to awaken with the dawn and greet the day with a cup of coffee. I was tired out and not a little angry at the situation. After a demanding week at work, I'd spent a restless night all scrunched up on a two-seater settee. Each time I had opened my eyes I saw Toby Jug's grizzled face anxiously staring down into mine as he lay stretched out on my chest. Now, both of us were glad to be outside in the cool, fresh morning air after the stuffy heat of the sitting room. I immediately began to reconnoitre the lay of the land and Toby Jug disappeared into the garden. As far as I could see, from looking up at the roof and the chimney stack, it was becoming increasingly serious since the swarm around the chimney had grown hideously in size and the sound from my bedroom had become an ominous drumming noise. Perhaps the message 'Come and join us' had gone out over the bee grapevine.

Having slept in my clothes and unshaven as well, I was in no way fit to face the outside world but I was just about angry enough to do so. Opening the garden gates I backed the car out of the garage and from nowhere was at once joined by Toby Jug who leapt on to the front passenger seat, obviously determined not to be left behind to 'guard the fort', especially since it was under attack. If the captain was leaving, then he wasn't going to be left behind. In times of adversity, Toby Jug believed that discretion was the better part of valour. His motto was: if danger threatened, then the safest place was behind me.

Heading down the A1 to Morpeth at speed, a journey of approximately eight miles, I had the usual difficulty in parking on a Saturday morning. Eventually finding a parking place in a shadowy tree-lined backstreet and leaving one window partially open for ventilation, I assured Toby Jug that I would soon be back. Then I headed off for the main thoroughfare to find a chemist.

The white-coated teenage assistant found my requests somewhat bizarre and hastily summoned the pharmacist, who treated my emotional outburst about the bees with remarkable professional detachment. By now a small crowd, drawn by the unusual nature of my request and the intensity in my 'lecture-room voice', had gathered near the pharmacy counter. When I turned to look at them none would make eye-contact. Obviously I sounded and looked like some kind of crank. The chemist nodded in an aloof manner and departed into his inner sanctum. Some moments later he emerged with a cylindrical container with enough poison to kill all the troublesome bees in Northumberland. Poor bees! But I was in desperate straits and the bees had the option of leaving. I didn't.

Hurrying back to the car, I was greeted with the not unusual sight of a group of children looking into the car at Toby Jug, who was enjoying the attention hugely. On the drive back I wondered what would happen if these tablets didn't work. What were my options? As far as I could see I didn't have any.

Arriving back at the cottage I immediately set about carrying out the pharmacist's directions. The bees were still in fervent occupation and some had even begun to swarm around the smaller chimney which served the kitchen. It was time for desperate measures. Since leaving the car, Toby Jug was nowhere to be seen. No doubt he would be watching from some concealed viewpoint of comparative safety as he reviewed the situation.

First of all, I vigorously stoked the fire until I could see smoke pouring out of the chimney but still the bees remained and were beginning to establish a second beachhead in the corner of the ceiling at the top of the stairs. I was puzzled by this at first until, with a raincoat over my head for protection, I crept a little way up the stairs and, peering through the banister supports, I saw to my horror that bees were streaming out from under my bedroom door. Any feeling of compassion for these creatures was quickly dispelled. From now on it was total war and I was not in the mood to take any prisoners.

Following the pharmacist's direction to the letter, I allowed the fire to die back to glowing embers and then threw two of the white tablets on to the red coals and immediately blocked the opening with a 'blazer', a heavy sheet of iron which had a handle attached to the outside, traditionally used in the coal burning cottages of the northeast to increase the draught up the chimney. Then I stood back and awaited the results. I was becoming increasingly fearful that if this didn't work I would have to abandon the cottage. To add to my alarm some stray bees had already invaded the room in which I was standing and were obviously reconnoitring the area for a full-scale invasion.

At first there were no discernible results from my latest gambit but after about ten minutes of anxious watching from the front lawn I could see that there were signs of a gathering of bees which soon covered the whole of the chimney breast and eventually spilled on to the roof itself. Elated at this development I dashed inside and added a further two pellets to the fire. The view from outside was heartening. A swarm of tremendous size had gathered on the roof, covering the whole area of the chimneys and the adjacent tiles. The sight was awesome. In effect the noise of agitated buzzing made by the swarm sounded like a muted chainsaw and caused a curious tickling sensation in the ears. Passers-by stopped to gape at the phenomenon. The buzzing of the bee swarm was so loud that it had already caused a number of the neighbours to gather in their gardens to watch the spectacle. From the comments people made, it was clear that we all hoped to see an exodus. There was an expectation it would be imminent. I certainly wished it to be so and feeling quite buoyant I began to exchange opinions with my neighbours. It was then that I noticed that Toby Jug, unseen by me, had somehow joined our expectant throng, but then cats have a way of knowing things.

The lift-off occurred somewhat later than we all thought. It was almost three hours after I had first put the chemicals on the fire. It was a sensational sight. It seemed that thousands of bees became airborne at the same time, almost as if guided by a single mind. In flight they formed an ominous black cloud which swirled in columns way high above the trees and over the river to eventually disappear from sight. A collective sigh of relief, possibly even a muffled cheer, from the crowd greeted their departure. Although magnificent in their own way I hoped that they would not invade any other hapless person's house. Several of my neighbours congratulated me on my good fortune in having got rid of the bees. One of them cheerfully advised me to get a bee guard around my chimney. Try as I might around the hardware stores in the weeks that followed I could not find out what a bee guard was. Perhaps it was a hoax.

I cautiously re-entered the cottage with Toby Jug following at a safe distance behind looking from side to side with his ears and his tail on high alert. Aware that there might still be some remnants of the invasion force who had not been able to escape, I explored the house gingerly at first and then with increasing confidence. There weren't any bees anywhere as far as I could tell. What was even more surprising was that there was no sign, either in the bedroom or the upper landing, that they had ever been there. It was mystifying. The look on Toby Jug's face mirrored my own amazement as we tentatively moved from room to room.

That night we were reminded intermittently of the bees' former presence as, sitting by the fire after dinner with Toby languishing in my lap, there came periodically a sszzzzzzzzzing down the chimney followed by a zitzzz as a dying insect landed in the fire. It seemed that those bees too overcome by the fumes to escape the chimney stack with the rest of the swarm were now expiring and dropping down the chimney. For the first few buzzes and zitzzes Toby Jug lifted his head, ears pricked intently, to identify what was happening, then as the sound became commonplace we both relapsed into a restful snooze amid hopes that the morrow would bring a happier day. The episode of the bee invasion was over and we could contentedly relax. It had been a harrowing experience.

It was the final day of the summer term at Alnwick College. The setting of examinations, the marking of exam scripts and the endless committee and qualification board meetings had served their ritualistic purposes to the full. Now, and for the next ten weeks, the college would be closed and the Duke of Northumberland's castle would belong solely to him, his family, the tourists and, of course, the ravens. I was greatly relieved to be going home to the peace and quiet of the cottage after the hectic term that had just finished. I arrived home to find one of my colleagues, Diane Forester, who taught Art and Craft Design, waiting for me at the entrance to my drive. As I got out of the car to open the gates she rushed forward and began speaking urgently as if she had no time to lose.

'Sorry that I didn't catch up with you at college,' she said. 'I got your address from the office. Could you do me a real big favour and look after my horse, Fynn, for the summer? She's no trouble really and I believe you rode her a few times when she was at Moorgate Stables.'

Somewhat taken aback by this full-frontal approach I stared at her with apprehension, while she had a look of anxiety doubled with desperation. She looked genuinely all hot and bothered. Obviously, she was experiencing some kind of emergency otherwise she wouldn't have come to me as we really didn't know each other at all well. In the meantime Toby Jug was pacing up and down, rubbing himself against my legs and trying to remind me that it was his dinner time. I invited Diane into the cottage and got the whole story whilst I fed Toby Jug.

The following day she was due to go on holiday abroad for several weeks with her family. Unfortunately, the arrangements for the care of her horse, a dark grey Connemara filly which I rode a few times before she bought her, had fallen through and someone at the college had suggested that I might be able to help her out. I could see that she was on the verge of tears as she sat on the edge of a kitchen chair clutching a handkerchief tightly in her fist.

'Of course I'll pay you for your trouble,' she began and I waved dismissively with embarrassment. I told her that as I didn't intend going away this summer I was prepared to look after her horse to the best of my ability. With that her eyes suddenly lost their intensity and heaving a sigh of relief she sat back in the chair and accepted the cup of tea I offered her.

Then she noticed Toby Jug who, having finished his meal, was busy washing himself. She leaned forward and stroked him but he wasn't sure of her and swiftly moved away to lie down by the door. I had noticed before that cats tend to avoid people acting nervously.

Toby Jug gave a piteous whine, and appeared on a branch just annoyingly out of reach.

Dirty and bedraggled, with the pathetic look of a waif, as I'd never seen him before.

Walking with Teby Jug in the Cheviot foothills in a rainstorm.

We fed the ducks and swans at Bolam Lake and wished them a 'Happy Christmas'.

'Fynn was very fond of the stable cats at Moorgate,' she said as she groped for something to say. Toby changed his mind and leapt on her lap for some strokes. He didn't stay there long, though, and I felt that Diane was much relieved because she commenced assiduously brushing down her light-coloured skirt and examining it for cat hairs and paw marks. I was relieved that she didn't find any as I gently nudged Toby with my foot out through the open patio door and into the garden. Then she changed back into hurried mode and, fishing in her handbag, handed me the keys to the tack room and a sketch map of the location of the field in Denwick where Fynn was stabled.

'I really am most awfully grateful,' she said. She'd got what she came for and didn't know how to leave without giving offence. I decided to help her out. 'You'll no doubt have a lot of packing and arranging to do,' I ventured.

Her smile gushed relief. Springing to her feet she grabbed her car keys from the coffee table and said, 'Yes I have. I must be off. Thanks for the tea.'

This must have been no more than a politeness since I noticed her cup was still full to the brim on the coffee table where I'd placed it. I followed her out to the car, slightly amused by her agitated manner. Before she sped away she called out to me from the open car window: 'Ride her just as much as you like. Regard her as yours for the next six weeks. Thanks again. Cheerio!'

Her inky blue-black Jaguar hummed as she drove away.

'Now what have I done?' I said, pacing the garden as Toby Jug frolicked around my feet. He loved these accompanied walks around the garden and was longing to show me the special places that he'd discovered that day, like the hedgehog's nest of dried grass and fern where she was rearing three piglets and the broken remnants of starling's eggs under the lilac tree. But tonight I was wrapped up in my own thoughts and didn't pay much attention. I had other things on my mind, like what was I going to do with a horse for the next six weeks.

The dawn next morning was so full of sunshine that it woke me by shining through my bedroom window at around five a.m. I find sunbeams seen through the leaves of the trees especially appealing in the early morning and the sight invited closer inspection. Once outside I sat for a while, enjoying my first mug of tea and the clean fresh air. It had rained overnight and as the breeze shook raindrops out of the trees they sparkled like jewels in the sunlight. The urge to get up and savour what promised to be a glorious summer day had been too strong to resist even though it was so early. Toby Jug was an exuberant early riser and always keen to be involved in everything that was happening. He was particularly excited in the morning whereas I took a while to surface. For my part I was thinking about the practicalities of caring for the horse and deciding what we could do together over the coming weeks to relieve the boredom of carrying out the repetitive chores of feeding, exercising and mucking out the stable as well as all the household and garden jobs in the cottage. Still, it was great to think that the day belonged to me and that I could forget about work for a few weeks.

Later that morning, accompanied by Toby Jug, I set off in the car to find out where in Denwick village the horse was waiting for us. The village is in reality a hamlet and travelling by car it is easy to bypass without realizing it. After driving to and fro several times, and making hasty consultations of the sketched map, I eventually found the entrance to a long field flanked by tall hedges of overgrown hawthorn and beech. At the far end of the field, under a huge spread of horse chestnut, stood Fynn in perfect pastoral repose.

After parking the car and leaving a more than slightly miffed Toby Jug shut inside with, as ever, the window slightly open for fresh air, I walked to the gate and tentatively whistled an invitation to Fynn. At the sound, she turned her head in my direction, took a momentary look and then resumed her relaxed pose. She obviously hadn't recognized me. Sighing with misgivings at the task ahead of me, I unlocked the tack room in search of a rope and bridle. Walking slowly down the field towards her, she again glanced my way, rolled her eyes and trotted off to a far corner of the field. This was going to be harder than I thought.

About an hour later, with sweat running off me, I led a roped, bridled and frisky horse up the field and tethered her to the stable door. By this time a frantic Toby Jug was jumping from one side of the car to the other in a state of apoplexy at being left out of the proceedings. Feeling guilty, I retrieved him from the car and introduced him to Fynn who gave a whinny of greeting but also surprise as Toby leapt from my arms and settled comfortably on her back just below the withers, between the shoulders. Fynn turned her head, gave Toby Jug a long look, snorted and bobbed her head up and down a few times in approval and then resumed standing quietly as I combed her tail.

'Well I never would have believed it,' I exclaimed to myself as the two of them obviously hit it off from the very beginning. Diane Forester must have been right about Fynn liking cats and I had thought she had just been making conversation. Sometimes the behaviour of animals really amazes me. The idea of Toby Jug taking so readily to a horse hadn't crossed my mind as a possibility but then he was so unusual that I should have expected it.

The rest of the day was spent with Fynn and I getting to know each other. I rode her around the field, schooling her to my way of riding and generally familiarizing us with each other. I left a confused and somewhat jealous looking Toby Jug to sniff around the stable and later to watch us forlornly from the roof of the tack room.

Back at the cottage that evening I was in good spirits, having enjoyed the day thoroughly. Fynn was a fine horse, gentle-natured and, once she'd got used to me, easy to handle. I like horses and horse-riding has always appealed to me. With Toby Jug resting peacefully on my lap I got to thinking and had a brilliant idea, or so I thought at the time. It was partly stimulated by the sense of freedom that holiday time brings on but also by the weather forecast on the radio that predicted a prolonged spell of good weather with high pressure systems coming our way. I found the desire to be outdoors and into the countryside an irresistible temptation. Nursing the idea secretly to myself I thought what a surprise it will be for Toby Jug when he finds out. Our life together would soon be taking a more adventurous turn.

My idea was to take Toby Jug with me on horseback to camp for a few days in the Cheviot Hills. I could take full advantage of the fine weather and also Diane Forester's offer to ride Fynn as much as I liked. It would also do me the world of good after spending so much time indoors at college on office administration. However, there would be some serious planning to do if the trip was to be a success. Transporting Toby Jug on horseback would present a major challenge but I thought I might have a solution if I did decide to take him with me. The alternative of leaving him at my mother's or a cattery was unthinkable. Anyway, he was sure to get wind of my intentions and if he thought he was going to be left behind he would be inconsolable. If it was possible, I wanted to have him with me. Life with Toby Jug was good fun most of the time and, after all, he deserved a holiday as much as I did.

Setting out to find the supplies I needed necessitated a quick visit to Rothbury, a market town situated over the moors from Alnwick. The main street in Rothbury stretches up a hill on each side of which are all manner of shops. I was looking for one in particular, an archaic leather goods shop, a veritable storehouse of Victoriana that sold antique and second-hand items, including old-fashioned objects for horses and carriages. I wondered if the shop would still be there or whether it would have been by now turned into a snack-bar or coffee shop. It seemed ages since I'd been across to Rothbury, which is such a picturesque town.

Thankfully, the shop was still in existence. After spending an hour or so rummaging amongst old street lamps, various bridles and saddles and even rat-traps, I found what I'd been looking for: a pair of large saddle bags of burnished mahogany leather with strong brass fasteners which I bought for the bargain price of £3.10 shillings. The prize find was a set of twin picnic panniers, in basket weave with leather lids, made to be carried by a donkey, which I reckoned could be adapted to stretch across the back of a horse in front of the saddle. They would be exactly right for packing some food and drink on one side and Toby Jug on the other as long as Fynn didn't have a tantrum. The panniers were covered in dust and cobwebs and there was a small hole in one of the baskets but I was delighted and cheerfully paid £1 each for them.

Leaving Rothbury behind and delighted with my finds, my next stop was the Army & Navy Supply Store in Alnwick where I equipped myself with a double size sleeping bag for extra comfort, and two lightweight survival tents with a free battery-powered hanging torchlight thrown in. I also bought a mess tin, a billycan and a set of 'field' cutlery. Now I was ready for what I hoped would be an adventure.

The night before we were due to leave I caught the bus from Alnwick across to Denwick and rode Fynn back to the cottage for the night. There I bedded her down with some hay and horse nuts and tethered her to an iron ring in the wall of one of the stone outhouses which was open-sided and in which she could find shelter if necessary. Toby Jug was fascinated by all these goings-on and made himself comfortable in the pile of hay near Fynn. For a while I thought he'd deserted me to spend the night by Fynn's side but when bedtime came around he hastened inside to join me as usual.

I slept only a few hours that night and mostly lay awake imagining everything that could go disastrously wrong with the trip. The sun again woke me and I lay dozing a while, listening to the morning birdsong which served to relieve some of the tension. I was nevertheless glad to be up and about at around six to complete the last minute preparations. I hate waiting about and was eager to get underway. The Horse Transport had been booked for ten that morning and was to take us as far as Alwinton to give the expedition a good start. It arrived an hour late and Fynn refused to go in the horsebox.

As a last resort I copied a trick I had heard from one of the Duke's grooms who was well practised in dealing with spirited horses. I covered her head with a towel, led her around at a quick trot and raced her into the cab. As I removed the towel she snorted hard and kicked the sides in temper but when I spoke quietly to her and stroked her neck she settled down to munch a few apples I'd brought her. Toby Jug had watched these proceedings at a safe distance but now climbed unbidden into the horse cab and sat atop Fynn's feeding trough. He could stay there I decided until we were ready to go.

Before departing I slipped Toby Jug into his harness and lead as a precaution and took him to sit up front with the driver and me. As we drove away we were waved off by a small group of infant-school children returning from a nature walk who had stopped with their teacher to watch us loading. I could imagine them having to draw a picture in crayons of what they had seen and I wondered what tales they would tell their parents that evening. Thankfully, I had been spared the attention of my neighbours who were all at work and who, I guess, might have been dubious about the advisability of embarking on such a trip.

Wending our way through the sunlit leafy lanes of rural Northumberland was so restful that I found myself unable to resist nodding off, especially since the driver was rather surly and not at all pleased at being given this particular job.

'You must be ruddy daft,' had been his only comment when I'd explained our trip to him. 'You with a horse and a cat right up the ruddy "sticks". Mad,' he added for emphasis.

I decided to ignore him. Meanwhile, Toby Jug had perched himself on top of the engine and gearbox cover inside the driver's cab and was happily surveying all he could see in between catnaps.

Alwinton is a small community in the heartland of rural Northumberland. It took us nearly two hours to reach the Rose and Thistle pub there, which was to be our starting point for the trek. The arrival of the horse-wagon proved to be a momentous event. The lunchtime regulars ambled out, pint glasses in hand, to view our arrival with slack-jawed disbelief. Having resisted going in to the horsebox, Fynn now refused to come out. The driver, exasperated beyond his tolerance level, swore and cursed as he attempted to move half a ton of stubborn horse by manpower alone. He failed miserably.

Somewhat angered by this show of brutality, and embarrassed by the sniggers of the onlookers, I determined to take over myself. Picking a handful of bruised apples from the supplies, I purposefully strode into the horsebox, closely followed by Toby Jug. Fynn slowly turned her head at our approach and, feeling much aggrieved, whinnied in self-pity. Feeding her an apple at a time, and holding her headband, I backed her out of the box to the cheers of the drinkers who eventually drifted back inside the pub. The driver, in a further show of anger, banged shut the doors of the horsebox and, with a sneer in our direction, drove off. I hailed his departure with a sigh of relief.

Toby Jug watched me in a curious mood from his seat on the fence as I loaded Fynn with our supplies. I could see that he was wondering why we were here and where we were going. I had no really firm ideas except for the site of our camp, which I remembered having seen on a country walk some years previously. I guessed it would still be there as little changes in these remote parts of the county. I did expect that we would have some fun along the way. In other words, the journey would unfold as we progressed, that simply was all I had in mind. Finally, everything was packed and with Toby comfortably settled in the left-side pannier, we set off with me leading Fynn towards our first objective. Apart from snorting hard and stamping the ground really hard with a foreleg, Fynn had accepted the indignity of having the panniers on her back but I didn't dare ride her until she became used to them. Like me and Toby Jug, she was anxious to be moving.

The field climbed away rapidly as we left the Rose and Crown behind us. With a few shaggy-haired Highland cattle and a light breeze to keep us company we climbed ever higher into the hills. It proved to be an excellent day, weather-wise, and I was soon sweating profusely. Casting off my anorak I searched ahead for the campsite I had in mind. Soon, but not early enough for my weary limbs and raging thirst, the ruin of a stone building appeared on the hilltop ahead of us. It was the remains of High Steads Youth Hostel which had been abandoned after a mysterious fire. At the sight of it Fynn, who was no fool, stretched her neck and moved forward at a thrusting trot and I struggled to keep pace with her. On reaching the ruin all I could do was slump on to the grass with a cool drink of water from my flask. Fynn wandered off to the side to drink from a stony burn which had gouged a deep channel down the hillside. Toby Jug, whom I had momentarily forgotten, emerged yawning from his pannier wondering no doubt why we had stopped. He lost no time in joining me on the grass, his eyes vertical black slits in the bright sunlight.

After a brief respite I felt obliged to get things sorted. Donning a pair of sunglasses against the glare, I tethered

Fynn to a rusty pole protruding from a crumbling wall and set about unpacking and making camp for the night.

On looking over the ruin I decided it would be too risky to camp within its walls and chose instead to pitch the tent in the lee of the building under a stunted hawthorn tree which had a most wonderfully shaped trunk, all rugged and gnarled. A product of nature's artistry, it was a delightful thing to look at. I placed the saddle-bags and panniers between the back of the tent and the trunk of the tree and covered them with a waterproof sheet. I fed Fynn some small pellets of food known as horse nuts and some apples, and Toby Jug a tin of his favourite cat food. For myself I unpacked some prepared meat sandwiches and a flask of hot coffee and, for later, I wedged a bottle of Moscatel de Valencia in the stream so that it would become refreshingly cold to bring out the full Spanish flavour. While the horse contentedly rested and Toby Jug hunted insects in the grass, I collected twigs and branches from a nearby stand of trees to make a cooking fire in the morning.

In the cool of the evening I saddled Fynn and rode off in search of the farmer whose hayfields we'd passed on the journey up to the campsite. Toby Jug seemed happy enough to scramble after us on the short grass as Fynn walked and trotted the short distance. As we came nearer to the field I could see that men were already busy loading hay so I was just in time. Thankfully, there were no dogs about and I was able to leave Toby Jug playing around while Fynn cropped the hay stubble and I went to talk to the labourers. The farmer and his two helpers were very friendly and when they heard where I was camped, offered to drop off a couple of bales at the camp before they finished for the night.

Returning to the camp proved to be a marvellous experience, which made all the tasks of the day worthwhile. As we topped a ridge, the sky enveloped everything around us in glorious colour, glowing with vivid reds and pinks intermingled with subtler shades of aquamarine and purple. I felt as if I was in another world, so enriching were the sensations of being at one with the landscape and the heavens above. Mesmerized by the view I could only stare. Fynn, of her own accord, came to a halt and stood motionless. Toby Jug stopped gambolling and settled down in the grass to be part of it, too. I gazed in awe at the scenic feast around us. No sound disturbed the perfect stillness. Man, horse and cat were enchanted by a vision of nature, which was primeval in essence. We remained for a long while, captivated by its splendour.

Back at the campsite I unsaddled and loose-tethered Fynn and had just finished rubbing her down when the farmer arrived with the hay bales. We exchanged pleasantries for a while during which he mentioned that he could let me have some fresh eggs and home-cured bacon in the morning if I wished. Accepting this unexpected bonus with pleasure, I paid him immediately and we bade each other goodnight.

'Look here!' he called as he went to start his tractor. And there was Toby Jug lying in easy comfort on the soft cushion the farmer used on the steel seat of the tractor. 'Should I take him with me?' he laughed as he stroked Toby Jug who responded in typical extravert style by rubbing his head against the farmer's tweed jacket and making throaty purrs.

'He's a bonny little thing,' he said affectionately as he lifted him down.

Spooked by the noise of the tractor starting up, Toby Jug abandoned his social graces and headed straight for my shoulder as I waved goodbye to the friendly man. Such friendliness was not uncommon in the countryside and made me feel most welcome and at home here in the hills.

After spreading a night's ration of fresh hay for Fynn I retrieved the bottle of Moscatel – pudding wine my grandmother called it – from the stream and unpacked the carefully wrapped wineglass I'd brought with me. Wine didn't taste the same to me if it was sipped from anything other than a well-formed wineglass. The setting sun suffused the amber liquid with dancing lights as I held the glass high before me to better appreciate the colour of the wine and to toast Mother Nature and the universe at large. One glass was all it took to start me nodding with tiredness. Partly undressed, I slipped into my sleeping bag and leaned back against Fynn's saddle which, in true cowboy style, was to be my pillow. I remember little of the night except for Toby Jug moving around the tent as he changed sleeping positions and some bird calls that added an exquisite wild tone to the whole experience.

The sound of hooves pounding the ground jerked me awake. Bleary eyed I squinted through a gap in the tent flap only to see a herd of sheep moving by the tent, guided by two sheep dogs and an shepherd waving his crook. It was 5.30 a.m.

'Country dwellers rise early, really early,' I muttered to nobody in particular as Toby Jug merely stretched and yawned without apparently once opening his eyes. Feeling stiff and crotchety after lying on the hard ground, I was glad to be up and about. Imagine my surprise to find a cardboard box containing half-a-dozen fresh eggs still with hen's droppings on them, four thick slices of home-cured bacon, wrapped in greaseproof paper and a free half pint of milk, all left as promised by the friendly farmer. And I hadn't heard a sound of his coming or going.

Glad to be standing and stretching after the cramped conditions of the tent I gazed around at the green hillsides. They were coated in a film of mist through which the pale yellow sun was just beginning to burn. Fynn lifted her head from her grazing and snorted a welcome. She seemed perfectly content to be here and had eaten all the horse nuts and most of the hay during the night. As I rubbed her muzzle and stroked her neck by way of saying 'Good morning', she looked more at ease in these natural surroundings than she had done yesterday. The air was exhilaratingly fresh, smarting my lungs with its coolness. There was no sign of movement anywhere except for a sudden wafting of wings through the sky above as a covey of partridges flew in the direction of the hayfield we'd visited last night.

Hunger drove me to work and after a few false starts I eventually had the fire going and a billycan of water from the stream was soon boiling cheerfully. As the bacon and eggs were reaching the ready stage Toby Jug emerged from the tent and after two or three affectionate strokes from me, he headed off towards a patch of bracken for his morning toilet. I ate my breakfast and drank coffee laced with plenty of the fresh creamy milk, all whilst sitting on a tree stump and being warmed by the morning sun. Toby Jug, having finished his own breakfast, was lying on the broken wall near to Fynn's head. They acted like old friends, glad to be near each other as if they'd been together for years. Nothing disturbed the serenity of that early morning which served to recharge me emotionally and gave me a healthy dose of peace.

My plan was to use the site as a base camp for a few days while I explored the hills and valleys beyond. Leaving the provisions out of sight inside the tent and trusting to luck that they wouldn't be stolen, I took one of the panniers and secured it on the right side of the saddle for Toby Jug. Finally, I filled my water bottle from the stream and the preparations for departure were complete. As we started off, with the hot sun on my back and Toby Jug for the moment happily scampering about alongside Fynn's left flank, I headed north towards a stretch of pine forest at the top of the Cheviot valleys of Ingram and Langleeford.

As Fynn jogged along, my eyes were filled with an abundance of green and brown hillsides, thick with bracken and rye grass as yet untouched by human habitation. I was riding through part of the last great northern wilderness, England's natural heritage, which was regretfully being gradually whittled away as the twentieth century progressed. This morning, however, I could only hope that these wild places would be preserved for future generations of people and animals to enjoy as we were now doing. I looked around for Toby and saw him intently investigating some droppings near a rabbit hole, acting as if it was the most natural thing in the world for him to be doing. Fynn walked with her head held high, her eyes roving the terrain ahead and her nostrils testing the air. As for me, I was in my element and felt vibrantly alive and contented to be here.

Soon we drew near to a forest of fir trees and I called Toby Jug and signalled for him to join me on the saddle. He hesitated momentarily, enthralled by his own explorations, but when I called again his common sense took over and he leapt neatly to my lap. Fynn whinnied in alarm at the intrusion. I patted her neck to comfort her and eased Toby Jug into the pannier after first attaching the lead to his harness. I wasn't sure what we would find in the wood and judged that Toby would be safer attached to me.

There were areas of deep shadow in the forest as we picked our way along well-defined animal paths which I assumed were deer tracks. Most striking of all to my senses was the all-pervading stillness of the thick conifer trees. I sighted a roe deer hind standing in a glade watching us through the trees, sunlight dappling her back and neck. Alarmed by our sudden presence she swiftly moved off, shepherding twin fawns before her. They made a magnificent sight and it bothered me that the scent of a human being scared her so much. As we progressed further into the forest the conifers bunched even closer together and I frequently had to hold on firmly and lie forward along Fynn's neck as we passed beneath thick branches. Sometimes Fynn had to rise up on her haunches and jump over fallen trees that barred our way.

'Not much life in this neck of the woods,' I said to myself, but I couldn't have been more mistaken.

As Fynn continued to move ahead warily, Toby Jug peeped apprehensively from his low position in the pannier, his nostrils flaring as he scented the delicious pines and conifers. I could see that his little body was bursting with excitement to explore these strange places. Several times I wondered about the advisability of turning back as the forest ahead grew more impenetrable. In a short while the thick wall of trees became an arched avenue and gave way to a variety of deciduous trees. There were huge oaks and ash, sycamore and beech which made the forest feel much more like an old English wood. Eventually, we arrived at a most welcome sight for weary travellers: a sunlit clearing, a grassy meadow deep in the forest. In relief I called a halt to give us all a well-earned rest.

I hadn't a clue where we were but it was such a liberating experience to be wandering at will, without having to care about the ordinary demands of life. I felt like a schoolboy playing truant. It was a delicious feeling. I loosened Fynn's saddle and let her go to enjoy the sweet meadow grass. As for Toby Jug, I could see he too wanted to be off exploring the woods but I didn't dare risk losing him here, so I lengthened his lead with a piece of rope which I tied to Fynn's saddle. Then as I was settling down to eat a bacon and egg sandwich made from the remains of breakfast, I was startled by strange bird calls which seemed to come from all around the meadow.

At first I could see nothing. The calls were different from anything I had ever heard, a kind of sharp metallic sound repeated over and over again. It was as if they were flying around us but able to use the camouflage of the tree foliage to stay out of sight. Some birds, of course, prefer to be heard but not seen.

Mystified, I looked around the clearing several times before I finally spotted what I thought was a budgerigar, only slightly larger. It had a red body with dark brown and green-shaded wings and a thick neck like a parrot. Once my eyes became more accustomed I could see several of the birds moving about in the fir trees around a swampy part of the meadow. There were some duller, olive-coloured birds as well, which I guessed might be females. They were coloured white on their lower backs and the white patch could be seen whenever they flitted from one branch to another. Watching them more closely I saw that they were tearing away at unripened conifer cones with hooked bills which resembled those of a parrot but were crossed. What an exciting find. These birds were not native to Britain. They were migrants, I was sure of that.

Then I realized what they were: I was witnessing a family group of crossbills at work. I had recently read about these birds who had been much in the local news in the mid-1950s. The article I read said that these birds were forced to leave their usual habitat in the more northerly regions of Europe and Russia when the cone crop failed. The birds had migrated out of necessity to the coniferous forests of Northumbria and were especially widespread in the

Kielder area. I recalled that a member of staff at the college, an enthusiastic bird-watcher, reported having seen some in the Rothbury woods. Here I was, sitting amongst a flock of them deep in Thrunton Woods, which seemed a thousand miles away from my cottage, having an experience of which some bird-watchers could only dream.

Keeping as still as possible I watched them feeding. They seemed too pre-occupied to bother about us. Nevertheless, I expect the rapt attention they were receiving from Toby Jug had not gone unnoticed. The sight of these colourful birds was for me an additional bonus on what had already been a special trip. It was also an endorsement of what I had long held to be true. Northumberland was a treasure trove of natural beauty enriched by the rare wildness of its flora and fauna. Just as I was thinking this, a red squirrel emerged from an aged oak only yards from us and began chittering at the crossbill invaders. My pleasure in that perfect afternoon was complete.

Later, we were riding through thick forest when Toby Jug went on full alert. He looked toward a particularly dense clump of trees nearby. Clearly he had heard or seen, not for the first time in our travels, something I could neither see nor hear. Abruptly, he turned to face me, gave a little cry and before I could react, sped off and was soon out of sight. As frequently happened, I was caught out by the speed of Toby's response. I started up in surprise and called after him to no avail. Fynn whinnied and snorted as if to say she too was mystified. 'That makes two of us,' I said as I tried to figure out what had caused Toby to run off like that. I asked myself if this could be a last goodbye, after all he had tried to communicate something beforehand. Was it perhaps the irresistible and inevitable call of the wild?

To go after him was impossible; it was already late afternoon and shadows were gathering. I would simply have to sit it out and wait for him to find me if he wanted to. I spent an uneasy night anxiously starting up at the slightest sound, hoping to see the grizzled black-and-white face I so loved. But it didn't happen. Facing the possibility of not seeing Toby again was very hard. I began to reflect that perhaps he had become bored with living with me, that he yearned for adventure rather than being shackled, however lovingly, to me. After all, he was no longer a kitten. His cat nature would lead him to think as a more independent entity. I began to question who indeed was the slave and who the master in this relationship. I felt as emotionally bonded to him as he no doubt felt to me. But if there was this symbiosis between us, why did he run off like that?

As time went on and it began to grow dark, I became racked with anxiety. I fed the horse and soaked her muzzle with a damp cloth. Then, feeling quite miserable and depressed, I decided I'd turn in for the night. I had neither eaten nor imbibed my customary glass of wine. I felt abandoned and just wanted Toby Jug to come back to me. I slept fitfully, tossing and turning. Half asleep in the forest I began to imagine the worst, no doubt influenced by my rather intimidating surroundings. But then I awoke with a start. I heard a noise close by: something big, very big, was trying to get into my emergency tent. My worst fear was that it might be an angry badger or other wild animal. Grabbing my torch, I took my courage in both hands and yelled 'Get away' as I unzipped the flaps and rushed out.

Whatever had been there had disappeared. I checked my watch. It was 2.30 a.m. and, of course, it was not yet light. I flashed my torch around, at first discerning nothing. Then I spotted two bright green eyes staring out from the undergrowth. It was a small animal carrying something in its mouth. Peering through the gloom my heart leapt as I recognized Toby Jug, who padded towards me and dropped a huge woodpigeon at my feet. He seemed extremely pleased with himself and I was so overwhelmed at his safe return that, like a parent, I couldn't decide whether to hug him or reprimand him. In the event I did neither; I just picked him up and cried with relief. He purred and meowed as if to say he was glad to be back. The woodpigeon was clearly meant as a gift for me. Perhaps Toby was also saying sorry he had left. Tomorrow we would be on our way but for tonight I put his harness on and attached the lead to my belt. I was taking no chances. There would be no more absences without leave in the depths of the forest. Actually, he seemed exhausted after his adventures and lay in his usual place across the top of my ankle and soon we were both in a deep sleep.

We rose later than we usually did the following morning and I accompanied Toby on his morning toilet and ablutions which he completed by rolling over and over in the heavily scented carpet of pine needles that covered the forest floor, luxuriating in the experience to the full. Then, saddling up with the tent and blankets tidily rolled up and tied on Fynn's back, we set off for the open country bordering the top end of the Wooler Valley. As we rode clear of the forest down a well-travelled bridal path, Fynn snorted and stamped, Toby Jug's little head turned from side to side and I thought here we go again, now what's this all about. Were we being watched? Any fears we had were soon forgotten because as we came closer I realized that we had somehow managed to make our way back towards our original campsite.

I could feel Fynn tensing for a good run which, after all, is what horses are meant to do. At first we cantered, the rocking chair ride, and then I let her have her head and we galloped with the wind in our faces and the sun at our backs. Toby Jug hunched down in his pannier in fear at the motion and the sound of the pounding hooves, his eyes fixed intently on me all the time. For my part I fervently hoped that Fynn, in her gallop, would not step into a rabbit hole. However, in double quick time we were back at camp without any mishaps to find that all there was well and the same as we had left it.

Before turning in for the night I sat looking around me at the landscape in the light from the setting sun with my customary glass of wine. The mood at our camp was restful as we three took the opportunity to unwind after the day's travel. I could hear the sound of Fynn munching contentedly in the background. Toby Jug stretched out comfortably by my side and I, at that moment, would not have wished to be anywhere else in the world.

There is a cadence to the sound of the wind in wild open spaces that has a musical pitch to it and the higher up the hills the more melodic it becomes. High up in the crags and over moorland the wind whines like massed violins, while down in the valley it lilts as it surges through the long grasses. Such harmony has a raw appeal and we three travellers, Fynn, Toby Jug and I, each in our own way, sensed its rare orchestrations. For the whole of the third day we heard only this eerie music as it coursed across the foothills and valleys of the Cheviot Hills. Lonesome birdcalls, many of which I didn't recognize, accompanied the creak and jingle of Fynn's saddle and harness. It was so quiet that at times I could even hear my own breathing above the sound of the wind and the muted snores of Toby Jug as he slept in the pannier.

Spiritually, it was very uplifting and it didn't matter that the day was dull with heavy grey clouds. We were mute witnesses, Fynn and I, to the wildlife of the hills and heather. We were able to observe all of this because we were just creatures moving across the terrain without threatening anything. A hare loped alongside us no more than ten feet away, curious as to whom we were. We suddenly came upon a fox devouring a rabbit and were given only the merest of cursory glances. There were the birds, rustic-feathered kestrel hawks plaintively crying 'KiKiKi' as they scoured the moors for rodents, while overhead some kind of buzzard soared, warily inspecting us. The dark-shaded figures of grouse skittered through the moorland scrub, darting sideways for refuge in the gorse as we advanced. All of them were wild creatures not partial to the human voice, creatures who usually try to keep themselves hidden from its invasive presence. But there were no human shouts and chatter to disturb the ambience of that day.

It was dusk when we got back to camp and after hastily caring for the horse and Toby Jug, I ate a quick meal of cold baked beans straight from the tin. It had been a splendid day and I felt pleasantly tired. Toby Jug ran amok, catching and eating moths, which as usual upset his stomach, and he came and vomited near me. Clearing away the mess I didn't have the heart to reprimand him because he hadn't been his normal chirpy self that day and I suspected that he might be homesick. Having had enough of the moths, he snuggled down next to me. I made a mental note to give him extra attention in the morning. Tomorrow would be the fourth day camping and we were running out of provisions. It was with regret that I realized it was time to pack up the camp and move on. It would take us at least two days to reach home.

Rising early, I spent a lazy morning under an overcast sky packing for the return journey. I swear I could smell rain. Fynn greeted me with a loud whinny and came forward for some strokes. She had become much friendlier, rather like a big dog, as we got to know each other better. She had almost finished her supply of hay and it would have to be horse nuts and whatever she could forage on the way back. The air had a clammy feel to it and I guessed it would pour down sooner or later. I unpacked my oilskin slicker and tied it behind the saddle.

Toby Jug seemed to be his old frisky self again as I watched him jumping at flies in the short grass. What a change there had been in him since the time that the professional opinion was that he would never get better, that he would die or at the very best be only a sickly runt of an animal. Here he was in the prime of health and happiness. He had coped with the demands of this camping trip with characteristic enthusiasm and had so far shown the resilience to deal robustly with new situations and novel experiences. I reflected that whatever challenges life threw at this little cat he always came up stronger and more confident. He showed strength of personality in every situation he encountered and I felt proud to have him with me.

It was almost midday before we were ready to move off on a course that would take us down by Greenside Pyke and into the Ingram Valley. For a while Toby ran alongside but soon tired and rode the rest of the way with the bottom half of his body in the pannier and the top half stretched across the front of the saddle. As we descended to the valley floor we cantered through swathes of wild flowers, not many of which I could name but I recognized Wild Comfrey and Herb Robert as well as the brilliant yellow patches of Celandines.

We stopped briefly by a large pool in a fast-running stream at the lower reaches of the valley. It proved to be a mistake. After I had unsaddled Fynn, she wandered over to the pool to drink. I wasn't paying much attention since I was opening a tin of beans for my lunch. The sound of loud splashing made me look up to see Fynn happily rolling in the pool watched by an attentive Toby Jug. Suddenly, Toby dived into the pool to join Fynn and, as he surfaced, was instantly swept away by the current. Shouting in alarm I scrambled to my feet and set off in hot pursuit. I tried to run fast but the last few days on horseback had jiggered my knees and in any case riding boots are not really suitable for sprinting.

Hobbling along I desperately searched the stream ahead for a sight of him but in vain. I was trying to look everywhere at once. Then I spotted him, a bedraggled dark figure at the edge of a bar of pebbles and stones which formed a confluence between two arms of the stream. Pulling my boots off took no mean effort but soon I was able to wade over the stream bed of slippery pebbles to reach him. He was still coughing and spitting water after his ordeal but, apart from being sodden, he was otherwise alright.

Back on land I dried him with my hand towel as best I could. Looking really sorry for himself he began the washing routine no doubt to groom himself back to normality. Meanwhile Fynn, curious as to what all the fuss was about, emerged from the pool, walked over towards us, shook water everywhere and managed to grind my can of beans under one of her hooves. It was the first calamity of the trip and I hoped it would be the last.

After a brief respite while the animals dried off, I ate my only remaining food, a bag of crisps, and then we continued our journey. As the afternoon wore on the cloud grew darker overhead and it began to rain, lightly at first and then it became a downpour. It took only seconds for me to don the waterproof slicker but I was already soaked. At least it served to cloak the saddle bags and panniers, one of which housed a subdued and half-drowned cat.

Leaving the valley behind we skirted the road wherever we could but were horn-blasted a number of times by unsympathetic car drivers. It was a miserable ride and it was with relief that the gaunt towers of Lemmington Hall appeared through the gloom.

The hall was used as a convent by the Sisters of Mercy who ran a residential facility there for girls with special educational needs. I had run an in-service course for the staff about a year ago and I fully expected that the good nuns would remember me and most probably offer food and shelter for the night. I rode around to the back of the hall where I knew there was a gatehouse entrance. By now the evening had turned really foul with a rising wind causing the rain to lash against us. A sharp-faced nun wearing spectacles peered around the edge of the door in answer to my knocking.

To reassure her I gave my name and asked to be remembered to the Reverend Mother. Then I explained my predicament and asked for help. In reply the door slammed shut without a word being spoken. I waited helpless, holding Fynn by the bridle, with the rain running down my neck under the cloak and through into my boots. In keeping with my mood and to add to my growing worries, Toby Jug began to wail, probably because the rain had dripped into his pannier and he'd been drenched enough. I felt the living embodiment of the saying 'As miserable as sin'.

Just as I was about to leave in despair to try to find some shelter in the woods, the door opened a crack and an unseen person directed me in a hushed voice to go to the gamekeeper's cottage.

Alerted no doubt by a phonecall from the hall, the gamekeeper was already standing in the doorway waiting for me, the light behind illuminating his huge frame and deerstalker hat. No pleasantries were exchanged between us as he guided me towards a row of outbuildings which he identified as stables and a gun room.

'Ye can bed down in the stable or the gun room as you like. I've unlocked the both,' he said in a gruff bass voice.

I turned to thank him but he'd vanished. I was beginning to experience a creepy sort of feeling at these turn of events, as if I'd entered a weird village twinned with Transylvania, inhabited by spectres. Light-headed with hunger and tiredness I wondered if his name could be Igor or Drakos and whether we would ever leave this place alive. Nonetheless, I was thankful for the shelter, meagre as it was, but there were no offerings of food.

The stables were bare but dry. Under the light from a single electric light bulb I lifted a damp Toby Jug out of his pannier and set him down on the cobbled floor. Swiftly unpacking and unsaddling Fynn, I made her as comfortable as I could and fed her the last of the horse nuts. Next I filled a pail of water for her from a tap in the yard, although I doubted whether she would need any after the soaking she had already endured.

The gun room offered about the same level of hospitality as the stables but I consoled myself with the thought that it was better than spending the night out in the woods. Spreading my sleeping bag over the long ridged wooden table, I slid in and fell asleep with the sound of Toby Jug washing himself yet again while I stupidly pondered why there were no guns in the gun room.

I awoke cold, damp and stiff minutes after six o'clock in the morning, having spent the night tossing and turning with every kind of ache imaginable in my back and knees. 'Well, it's nobody's fault but yours!' I told myself as I decided to start on my way as soon as possible. We were on the last leg of the journey and I expected to be home by nightfall at the latest. Toby Jug had found a warm place for the night on a torn cushion which was lying on a bench under the barred window. Trust a cat to find the best berth, I thought. He raised his head, looked up at me and promptly went back to sleep. Fynn, on the other hand, was happy to see me and I had her saddled and packed up very quickly. Toby was reluctant to go back in his pannier but settled down when I stuffed a dry sweater in the bottom for him to lie on. I stroked him and told him gently that we would soon be home and that he had to stop his moaning and make the best of things. Whether he understood me or not, the simple reprimand had an effect because there was no more wailing or awkwardness from him for the rest of the journey.

I left Fynn standing in the yard whilst I walked over to the gamekeeper's cottage to thank my host. The upper part of the country-style door was open and I could smell coffee and breakfast. The gamekeeper, a florid-faced man wearing the same hat I'd seen him in last night, sat at a kitchen table in his braces and a collarless shirt with his sleeves rolled up to reveal hairy arms and hands like those of a boxer. In front of him lay a huge plate of bacon, eggs, sausage and fried bread, together with a steaming cup of coffee. My mouth watered and my stomach rumbled in torment at the sight. His wife, a thin woman wearing a flower-patterned pinafore, caught sight of me and came over to the door. I thanked them and asked if there was any charge. At this the gamekeeper glanced over at me and said: 'Y'ed best be leaving a couple a quid for the lad to clean up after ye.'

Having only offered to pay in jest I found myself blushing and having to rummage about in my clothing for the money. After paying I sensed that I was being a nuisance and bade them goodbye. There was no response and I have never been back.

The morning was dull but dry, although I had to be careful on the roads which were slippery wet after the storm. Having crossed Glanton Pyke and passed through the village the evening before, I was looking for the start of the old railway line from Alnwick which had to be close by. Finding a way around some fields under cultivation, I located the line at last. Fynn must have recognized it from her days at the riding school because she moved along at an eager trot. By ten in the morning we were on the outskirts of Alnwick and home was a mere ten miles away. It had taken less time than I had expected.

Circumventing the town we followed the bridle path through the pastures, an area of grazing land with common access owned by His Grace, the Duke of Northumberland. Riding alongside the River Aln, with Alnwick Castle in the background, my spirits rose again and I looked forward happily to journey's end. Soon we crossed over the road to Boulmer and followed the Aln until we forded it within sight of Lesbury and Alnmouth. This was the long way round but I had to find a route that crossed riding country or suffer the hazards of riding along busy roads. After leaving Alnmouth behind, the trail headed inland and we were soon passing through the woods at Low Buston and in a direction due south again for Guyzance.

Pausing to give Fynn a breather and a chance for Toby Jug and I to stretch our legs, I took time out to admire the multicoloured mushrooms and toadstools the rain had brought out. They stretched between the trees like a carpet in strikingly beautiful hues of red, green, yellow and gold. Toby Jug made a brief foray amongst them and scattered some of their fleshy tops but swiftly turned away at the obnoxious smells they gave off. Perhaps some of them were the so called 'magic mushrooms', much prized among the drug fraternity for their hallucinogenic properties. As for the rest, they'd be deadly poisonous in spite of their bonny colours.

Mounted up again and with Toby Jug safe in his pannier, this time with the lid open so that he could lean on the edge and look out, we pressed on. By the early evening we caught sight of Foxhelliers Farm which meant that Owl Cottage lay only a mile beyond. We covered the remaining distance at a restful pace.

Unlocking the gates to the drive it was comforting to see that nothing had changed except that the grass of the lawn was longer. No doubt Fynn would soon take care of that. I led her into the garden and tethered her to the ring in the wall. Toby Jug leapt down out of the pannier, raced up the garden and climbed halfway up a beech tree for the sheer joy of being back. We were home again and glad of it.

The inside of the cottage seemed too enclosed and stuffy for my liking after the days spent out of doors. Strolling into the bathroom I got the shock of my life. There confronting me was the stark figure of a baddie from a low-budget Hollywood cowboy film. It took me long seconds to realize that I was staring at the mirror image of myself. The apparition that stared back at me was dishevelled, with dark hair covering a grimy face and five days growth of beard, dressed in a scruffy lumberjack-style shirt, mud-spattered jeans and dirty riding boots. No wonder the nun at Lemmington Hall had refused to fully open the door. I must have been a frightful sight in the semi-darkness, standing beside a bedraggled horse with a cat wailing in the background.

Two hours later Fynn had been rubbed down and brushed, supplied with hay and water and given a welcome home ration of horse nuts. Toby Jug had also been brushed and groomed and given one of his favourite meals. In addition, the figure in the bathroom had metamorphosed into a clean-shaven, well-scrubbed and fresh-smelling human being. Eating the first cooked meal I'd had for days was delightful and the glass of good wine to follow soothed away the aches and pains that are an inevitable side-effect of prolonged horseback riding. I reflected that I'd embarked on a rather foolish escapade with overtones of a schoolboy adventure. I shuddered to think what might have happened had I fallen and been badly injured or if Fynn had broken a leg. And what if I'd lost Toby Jug, drowned in the stream at Ingram Valley? But now that we were all safe and sound and I was in my cottage sitting comfortably in front of a warm log fire, my perspective on the camping trip became rosier. Overall, I had to admit that I'd had a wonderful time and I was glad that I'd taken the opportunity, despite the risks.

The next day we did very little. Fynn ate hay and cropped the grass; Toby Jug wallowed in sleep and arose only to feed and make a trip outside; I lay about reading, thinking and just watching the birds in the garden from a lounger in the conservatory. It would be time soon enough to resume the normal pace of life but for now we rested and whiled away the time in blissful abandon.

By the end of the week I had returned Fynn to her field in Denwick, done numerous household chores and attended to the garden. Everything was back to normal. Throughout the holiday period, whilst she was still my responsibility, I visited Fynn every day and took her riding three or four times a week. On the days when I didn't ride her I took Toby Jug with me, the two animals seemed to have become even closer since the camping trip. I was kept busy mucking out the loose box, loading hay and cleaning the water trough. The sight of Toby Jug on Fynn's back, sitting in little red hen-style, whilst Fynn moved around the field cropping the grass or stood dozing under the horse-chestnut tree near the bottom of the field, dumbfounded me. After a few weeks of this routine it mystified me how Fynn's owner, my colleague Diane Forester, with her coiffured hair and long, painted fingernails, could manage to do all this and look so well groomed.

In the days following our camping trip I gradually became aware that Toby Jug had changed. He looked and behaved differently somehow and then I realized what it was. He'd grown up. He was no longer a kitten. With my overprotective attitude towards him I subconsciously still thought of him as vulnerable but in fact he was fast maturing into an adult cat with independent airs. As Toby Jug grew in confidence he liked to roam further and further afield when he was not with me. Although I valued his freedom and independence as a cat, I couldn't help worrying about him whenever he didn't come quickly to me when I whistled and called. He loved the nearby woodland copses where he could prowl in tune to nature's call of the wild and I respected that. But the downside to a cat living and hunting as a wild creature is that the cat can, in turn, be hunted as a wild creature. Cats do seem to arouse more than a fair share of the violence meted out towards animals, even by humans, never mind dogs and foxes.

With all of this in mind, and because Toby Jug was so precious to me, I wanted to guard him from the world of hurtful happenings. Still, I had to learn all over again that a cat will go where a cat wants to go. Truly, the world is a cat's oyster. I had to rid myself of the tendency to think of him as being different and more vulnerable because of his poor start in life and because of his size. Toby Jug was, day by day, teaching me that he had his own agenda and he was simply asserting his rights by sometimes straying away from our home environment. I recognized and respected this but continued to worry. There was an element of foreboding about my feelings for Toby Jug's safety which on two occasions proved to be correct. One such incident was to rankle sorely in my mind for a long time afterwards.

AUTUMN

In autumn the salmon return to the upper reaches of the River Coquet to spawn. It is especially inspiring to witness this annual event which is part of the impressive and unbelievable range of intuitive behaviour laid down by nature in every fish, animal, bird and insect. It is impossible not to be impressed by the magnificent fish that have travelled hundreds of miles through the oceans to return to the river where they were born.

The weir on the Coquet is at a place where the river bends. It is sheltered by deep woodland on either side of the river bank and the river runs over gravel beds clearly visible in the sunlight. Sitting here is the best place to watch the salmon jumping. They hurl themselves over the weir in a seemingly impossible feat. Miraculously, most seem to make it and swim off up river until they meet the next obstacle.

Once I took Toby to see this wonderful event. It was a night when the moon was full – a wonderful night to be out enjoying the night air and the starry sky. Toby was in his element. We arrived at the weir and found a fisherman working the river. He seemed quite surprised to see us and smiled as he told me that salmon do not leap at night. I felt somewhat humbled but I had learned something. So instead, Toby Jug and I sat on the riverbank, taking full advantage of the ambience and occasionally I shone my torch on the water to illuminate the outlines of the salmon gathering below the weir, waiting for dawn to take the next step on their journey of life. Some were very large; all looked silvery in the torchlight. They swam around in a leisurely fashion, swaying as they moved. They seemed to be saving their energy for the final effort that lay ahead.

It was with a mixture of fear and fury that I found Toby Jug in a state of abject terror on November the 5th, Guy Fawkes' Night. The day had started with a fine crisp autumnal morning and after feeding I let him out for his morning stroll. I was working at home that day to finish an article in time to meet an editor's deadline. Whenever I spotted him, Toby Jug was happily playing in the garden amid the gathering piles of fallen leaves which were being enticingly swept about by a rising wind.

Around 4.30 p.m. I could hear fireworks parties starting in the village and there seemed to be more bangs and rockets zooms than normal. Toby Jug had never heard fireworks before and I was sure that they would startle and probably frighten him. I went outside and called his name. Normally, he would shoot towards me, especially since it was time for his evening feed. But there was no sign of Toby Jug in spite of my whistles and calls. I went back inside the cottage thinking he would soon return. Sometimes, he would suddenly appear on a window sill, looking in towards me and crying for me to open the door.

As time passed it grew dark and I began to get worried. I started to search for him in earnest. I looked in the outhouse with an opening in the wall where he was able to gain entry if I wasn't at home. Inside was a large linen basket with a thick woolly blanket for comfort but he wasn't there.

Just then a man from further along the road, whom I slightly recognized, was passing with his black Labrador. He stopped by my gate, looking red-faced and angry. 'You know,' he said, 'there's some young 'uns throwing fireworks into a garden. They've scared something up a tree, must be a squirrel or cat, and when I told them to stop they threw a banger at the dog. The young brats! I'd like to give them a jolly good hiding. Their parents must be morons.'

And with that he strode off without waiting for a reply, thumping his walking stick angrily into the ground to emphasize his feelings, with his dog following meekly at his heels.

My blood turned cold at the thought that it might be Toby Jug up that tree. I ran along the main street where I came upon a rowdy group of youths who were indeed throwing fireworks into the old vicarage garden. One of them, encouraged by the shouts of the others, was balancing on the garden wall and throwing fireworks up into the higher branches of an ancient oak tree that grew in the corner of the garden.

'Get ready to grab it if it falls,' one of them yelled just as I arrived panting and furious. I can't recall what I shouted at them, I only remember that I stormed into their midst, arms flailing and shoulders thrusting them aside, I charged at the big fellow on the wall knocking him into the garden and then I turned on them like an enraged bear. I was furious at what they were doing to some innocent animal, especially as it could be Toby Jug. Not surprisingly, they fled and left me drenched in sweat and hot with anger.

My heart was thumping so fast that I was shaking with emotion and needed to rest against the wall for a while until I calmed down. I wasn't accustomed to having aggressive confrontations and the whole business was upsetting. Turning to the tree I peered up into the branches. I could see nothing except dark patches among the twisted limbs which were still partly hidden from the streetlight by autumn leaves not yet fallen.

Just then a woman I recognized came out from her cottage across the road. She was at pains to tell me that she'd been terrified by the youths, who had thrown firecrackers into her passage way and burnt patches on her rug, and that she had telephoned the police. She went on to say that they deserved being chased and that I had done the right thing and that she hoped the little cat up the tree was all right.

My worst fears were confirmed. It had to be Toby Jug. Desperate to see he was safe but not yet absolutely sure it really was him up the tree, I clambered on top of the wall and softly called for him. A man, who the woman hailed as Andy, appeared and asked if it was my cat up the tree and would I like to borrow his ladder to have a look. Since there was still no sight of Toby Jug I accepted his kind offer. While he went to get the ladder, the woman, who identified herself as Jenny Croger, volunteered some more details which convinced me it was Toby Jug up there.

She said that she had watched the gang throwing lighted fireworks into the doorways of some of the other cottages and then she and Andy, her husband, had seen a black cat with white paws running along the path. The youths had chased it up the tree. They were trying to frighten it down when I came along.

'Is it yours?' she asked just as Andy arrived with the ladder.

'I think so,' was all I could say.

I thought guiltily that Toby had probably been running towards the cottage in answer to my calls and whistles and been waylaid by that gang.

'It'll not come down you know!' she said. 'Not with all

this going on.' She indicated with a nod of her head the sky over the treetops which was being illuminated at intervals by the flare, whoosh and bang of rockets. 'I've seen cats stay up trees for days on end,' she ended sourly as Andy and I manoeuvred the ladder over the wall and up against the tree trunk.

Andy steadied the ladder and Jenny watched from a safe distance with her arms folded and her head shaking doubtfully. I braced myself and began climbing up towards the crown of the massive oak that was shrouded in deep shadow. I have never been particularly good at heights – in plain terms they frighten me – and I have had to fight this fear on numerous occasions in my life. Now was such an occasion.

'Careful you don't fall!' Jenny called, which only made me feel worse.

As I balanced precariously on the ladder it began settling into the soft earth of the garden and I felt in imminent danger of crashing down into the street below. Eventually, and with increasing trepidation, I reached the top of the ladder and took hold of a thick branch for security. Straining to see in the semi-darkness of the tree foliage I could make out nothing in the form of a cat or anything else. From below, Andy and Jenny kept up a constant stream of questions as to whether I could see anything. Then I heard Andy tell Jenny to go and get a torch. That's a splendid idea I thought; why hadn't I thought of that? At that instant Toby Jug gave a loud-pitched piteous whine and appeared on a branch above my head, annoyingly just beyond my reach.

I called repeatedly to encourage him to come down further but he lay along the branch, apparently fearful of moving any lower. He simply stared at me and it looked as if he was not going to come down of his own accord. Levering myself yet higher by standing with one foot on the top rung of the ladder, I made a desperate lunge and at last managed to clutch Toby by the scruff of his neck. I hauled him towards me. He instantly fastened his claws deeply into my sweater and clung on for dear life. I would have fallen several times if it hadn't been for Andy steadying the ladder. Clinging desperately to each rung as I descended, feeling scared but triumphant, I at last reached the bottom. Almost at the same time Jenny arrived breathless with the torch. Thanking them both profusely for their kind help I scurried back to the cottage, holding a shocked and trembling Toby Jug.

Back in the safety of the cottage I began to relax with what I thought was a well-deserved glass of cognac, but Toby Jug was still scared. He wouldn't drink his milk, he wouldn't eat his meat – he simply wanted to huddle close into my side. He couldn't stop trembling. I stroked and soothed him as best I could but the sound of loud bangs from rockets and other fireworks even permeated the thick walls of the cottage and Toby would go into shock again. It took two days for him to regain even a semblance of his old self and then he stayed by the immediate surroundings of the cottage, slipping out only for calls of nature and hurrying back to the safety of his home.

That night I sat there thinking how awful it is that irresponsible youngsters can sometimes terrorize neighbourhoods in the way I had just seen. Not only was I concerned about my cat, who'd been frightened out of his mind by a gang using fireworks, but I also felt both saddened and outraged by the events that night, including the vandalizing of Jenny and Andy's cottage. She told me later that the police failed to respond to her call.

Toby Jug never seemed to recover from his terror of fireworks after his experience that night. Even a motorcycle backfiring could send him into a spasm of fear. I have heard that some dogs and horses have been similarly affected.

As the autumnal days set in and the trees began to display their foliage of lemon, golden brown and orange hues, Toby Jug began to recover his cheeky, cheerful personality although he didn't wander as freely as he once did. Not for a while anyway. One particularly fine morning I sat out in the garden with my morning mug of tea, taking in the air and reflecting that autumn is my favourite season because it is a time for contemplation. All the rush and push of spring and the hurly-burly of summer give way to a calm harvesting of nature's bounty. There is an excitement about autumn as previous efforts to grow reach completion and there is a pause before the change over to winter. I watched the early morning sun slanting through the trees turning the dew drenched grass to a silvered carpet of light. The house martins were getting ready for the long journey south. Above my patio area, wing-strengthening exercises of take-offs and landing were being performed in earnest whilst swarms of multicoloured butterflies were driving Toby Jug to distraction.

Later that morning I set off along some local woodland paths, thickly carpeted in cinnamon-coloured leaves, towards a small lake where I knew there'd be lots of large fir cones at this time of year. When burned in an open fire the cones give off a delicate aroma of pine which is extremely pleasing and fills the cottage for days with their natural scents. I also expected to gather some blackberries and had brought along a small bucket for that purpose.

After a somewhat nervous start to the walk because of his recent experience, Toby Jug soon began to respond to all the woodland smells and sounds by running here and there, sniffing and mock-pouncing on piles of fallen leaves. On nearing the lake, which is set in a hollow surrounded by trees, I was surprised by a sudden heavy 'clap clap' beating of wings as the wild ducks who lived there took off in abrupt alarm. The clatter made by the ducks did nothing to help

Toby Jug's nerves and he froze in momentary panic. The ducks didn't usually do that and I wondered why they were so afraid now. I had often visited the lake to feed the ducks scraps and even when they were nesting eggs they were never disturbed by my presence. What had changed?

That morning the lake was resplendent in a myriad of autumn tints and hues at once both familiar and refreshingly new to me. The area had always been a place of peaceful beauty which had an aesthetic of calm all of its own. Looking around, I saw it had become the focus of a meaner spirit. Notices everywhere were nailed to some of the magnificent old trees, They said: 'KEEP OUT'; 'PRIVATE PROPERTY'; 'TRESPASSERS WILL BE PROSECUTED'; 'PRIVATE SHOOTING'.

I also noticed with disgust the used shotgun cartridges scattered about on mounds and in newly dug shooting trenches. It was with a feeling of extreme disquiet that I realized why the ducks had fled at our approach and why I would never come back here again. I turned for home, with my hopes of a happy afternoon spent gathering fir cones and blackberries in communion with nature dashed. I was sick to my stomach at the way some people so abuse our natural treasures which I believe belong to everyone to admire and preserve. I muttered bitterly to myself all the way back with Toby Jug running alongside to keep up with my angry pace and giving me quizzical sidelong looks as he tuned into my changed mood. I subsequently learned that the lake and adjoining wood had been acquired by a property developer who leased it out to shooting parties. Sometime later I heard with relish that the ducks had abandoned the lake and were nesting up river instead.

During the half-term college break, I turned my attention to various jobs that needed attention around the cottage. I decided it was time to dig up the potatoes I had grown in my vegetable garden. I could give some of these, along with other vegetables, to St Michael's Church for their imminent harvest festival service. Happening upon a dry spell of weather during the week's break, I started digging up my crop. It was a golden autumn day, full of sunshine and warm breezes, just as I imagined an Indian summer should be. Toby Jug was as usual dogging my footsteps, wanting to be involved in everything I did. He felt obliged to give an investigatory sniff at everything I unearthed but would at times wander off in boredom to chase late summer butterflies, only to return and stare fixedly at the spot where I was digging. I would then drop the potatoes into a large bucket of water to clean them.

As the day wore on it grew warmer and I began to sweat profusely. Leaning on my spade for a brief rest I decided to shed my T-shirt. When I turned round, to my astonishment, I saw that Toby Jug had climbed into the bucket and was sitting on the potatoes, up to his neck in water. I was flabbergasted. Never had I witnessed anything like it before. I thought that cats and water did not mix but the heat had perhaps become too much for him and he had obviously decided to take a bath.

As I stared at him incredulously he leapt out of the bucket, shook himself rather like a wet dog and then settled near my feet. All genetics aside, as a Maine Coon Toby Jug really did have characteristics which were remarkably similar to the racoon, including being an decent swimmer when the need arose. Then I remembered how he had jumped into the stream at the Ingram Valley and nearly drowned in an attempt to join Fynn, but the force of the current had been more than he could manage. As the afternoon wore on I noticed him several times climbing into the bucket of water to cool off. He also started rooting in the bucket with his paws for potatoes which he then played with on the grass. I was still learning more about this cat every day.

Later that week I bought some fibreglass material to insulate the roof of the cottage. On a cold morning, when the sunny weather of the previous weekend was but a distant memory and nature was blowing up a wet storm, I opened up the attic and began the tedious and tricky job of laying the rolls of insulation material. I had been told that it would reduce my heating costs significantly by trapping more of the heat inside.

Toby Jug, as usual, was interested in what was going on and insisted on climbing the ladder into the attic area. I hadn't thought cats could climb ladders. I left him to prowl around while I was laying the obnoxious material which kept prickling the skin of my hands and knees and which Toby Jug, after just one encounter, studiously avoided.

Suddenly, a crisis developed when Toby Jug disturbed a pipistrelle bat in hibernation somewhere amongst the eaves. Realizing that he was about to catch it I made a desperate lunge and grabbed his tail before he could move in for the kill, or more likely to play with it as Toby Jug was not the killer type. Sadly, the end result for the bat would have been the same so I pulled Toby away from the corner of the attic and as I did so he dug in his claws and dragged out a wrapped bundle tied in old fashioned farmer's twine. It was covered in cobwebs and dust from the roof and I doubted whether it had seen the light of day for a long time. I pulled Toby Jug back to me by his tail and severely chastised him. Giving him an admonitory smack on the rump I sent him unceremoniously down the ladder. The bat had escaped unharmed due to my quick headlong tackle which meant, however, that now my whole body was covered in prickly fibreglass strands.

Feeling itchy all over and very uncomfortable I climbed down from the loft to change my clothes before attempting to finish the job. On my way to the bathroom I saw Toby Jug sitting on the staircase windowsill with his back deliberately turned to me to show that he was in a huff. Later, having completed laying the insulation in double quick time to protect my skin from further ravages, I remembered the bundle which Toby Jug had inadvertently found. Finding it again I carried it downstairs and unwrapped it on the kitchen table. To my great surprise it contained a primitive percussion shotgun belonging, I imagined, to the era of black powder and lead shot. It was a handsomely made weapon, with a reddish walnut stock and a ramrod aligned under the barrel. Where the stock met the barrel there was a silver mounting built into the wood with the name 'Braithwaite' inscribed on it. I was interested in this gun as a relic of the ways in which the inhabitants of my cottage in the early nineteenth century had lived and I decided to try to find out more about my find, or more precisely, Toby Jug's find.

Subsequent research at the City Library in Newcastle identified the gun as having been manufactured between 1770 and 1815. Further investigation in Alnwick's library revealed that, around the time of the 1830s, the area where my cottage is located was ruled over by a local squire who leased the land from the Duke of Northumberland. The land was in turn leased to tenant farmers who employed labourers to work their fields and care for the livestock. The farm labourers and their families would be housed in what were called 'tied' cottages as part of the employment contract. Whilst I hate the idea of hunting and shooting for sport, I can understand how these poverty stricken farm labourers would need to kill wild game birds and animals in order to feed their families and there is no shame on them for that. If caught, the penalties imposed by the autocratic landowners, who were often also the local magistrates, could be extremely severe and in some cases the poachers paid severely for their misdemeanours. Whoever lived in what was now Owl Cottage had probably secreted away his shotgun to avoid prosecution and the subsequent loss of his livelihood and home.

In the last century the area in which I live must have been teeming with wildlife ripe for poaching, as even now the place abounds with living creatures. The River Coquet remains a prime fishing water which is strictly supervised by the Anglers' Association with an appointed bailiff. From the ancient stone bridge in Felton, just 200 yards down from my cottage, it is possible to catch a glimpse of salmon, sea trout and more often brown trout as they leisurely wend their way upstream. While in the fields and woods adjacent to the river, there is an abundance of hares and rabbits, always prime targets for the local, as well as the itinerant, poacher.

Both at nightfall and in the early dawn I have often caught a glimpse of wild roe deer as they move along the wooded parts of the river banks. Once, during a walk in the early summer with Toby Jug on a harnessed lead, I met a fisherman who pointed me towards a hollow among the fir trees where a hind had hidden her fawn. Toby was immensely interested in the fawn and it was lovely to see the two animals as they touched noses without any fear of each other. The creature couldn't have been more than a couple of days old and it looked up at me with large amber eyes, for all the world just like Bambi in the Walt Disney film. I continued my walk and when I returned I looked for the fawn again but it had gone, although Toby kept sniffing around the ground where it had been as if he could find out through his nose exactly what had taken place.

After Toby had discovered the gun, I sought him out. He was sitting at the kitchen window watching the bird-table and chittering with rage at the blue caps and chaffinches who were noisily flying to and fro. He was clearly upset because I had smacked him when he was only playing and he obviously didn't understand the reason why. I rarely had to discipline Toby in any way and, although I had really only tapped him lightly, I had upset his feelings and he wouldn't look my way. I sought to redeem myself somewhat in his eyes by opening a small tin of red salmon for his tea as a gesture of friendship and as a reward for finding the gun, even if it was by accident. Toby Jug accepted my peace offering and friendly relations were restored.

As for the gun, I hung it from the oak beam embedded above the stone lintel of the fireplace and regarded it as a charmed survivor of the area's past. And there it stayed. I wouldn't have dared fire it even if I knew how since it would probably have blown my head off, but it was a fitting reminder of olden times. Whenever I looked at it I was reminded of the people who lived a very different kind of life from mine between these stone walls and who warmed themselves from the very same fireplace in front of which Toby Jug and I passed away many happy hours.

Some days after this incident, Toby Jug disappeared, although the two events were not related. He wasn't there when I returned home from the college and he didn't appear at all that evening. Unable to eat my tea or relax, I searched everywhere including the most unlikely places a cat would go. As the evening wore on without any sight of him my worry grew to a deep seated fear that tore at my mind. I imagined the worst that could have happened to him and my fantasies became even more fevered as the time ticked away.

Eventually I left the cottage to yet again make a search by torchlight of the fields and copses surrounding the cottage. I knocked on neighbour's doors to ask them if they had seen him, prevailed upon them to open outhouses and garages in vain searches and at last arrived at the bar of the

Northumberland Arms in a state of physical and emotional exhaustion. None of the assembled drinkers had any news of a missing black-and-white cat but some had woeful stories of pet animals that had gone missing without trace and had never been seen again. A feeling of sickening dread overwhelmed me and the landlord, sensing my despair, offered a complimentary glass of whiskey. The bar talk returned to more mundane events, albeit more hushed, and I was left in a solitary state at one end of the bar to dwell on my fears.

Suddenly my ears pricked up at a mention from the far end of the bar that the Percy Hunt had been active in the area during the morning. It appeared that several foxes had been caught by the hounds which had coursed through the local farmlands. Faces tautened and eyes lowered at my avid questions as to whether foxhounds ever savaged cats.

'I've seen hounds on the scent in a full run take anything in their path. Once they savaged a sheep dog that got in their way and it had to be put down,' said Les an ex-game-keeper and local savant.

Feeling really sick at heart I hastily left to return home and nurse my grief. There was no sign of Toby at the cottage and, too tired to search any more, I lay down on the settee and fell into a fitful sleep.

Nothing had changed by the morning and feeling desperate without Toby Jug I set off for work with a heavy heart. On my way home that evening I left printed notices in the Post Office and local shop offering a reward for any news of my cat. The cottage was a bleak and lonely place without him and, although I made every effort to keep busy, I couldn't stop thinking about Toby Jug and wanting at the very least to know what had happened to him. I tried without success to stop imagining him being torn to pieces by foxhounds but the images prevailed. I couldn't bring myself to remove his dishes and his basket but every time I saw them I experienced denial, a surge of unreasonable hope that because they were still there he was bound to somehow return alive. I also remonstrated with myself for the odd times that I had reprimanded him for doing something wrong, as I had done just a few days earlier. I looked for him again before I went to bed and again in the morning after a poor night's sleep. There was still no sign of him. I missed him terribly.

On my way to work I called into the Running Fox for my morning paper. Just as I was leaving, Helen, the shopkeeper, called me back.

'Betty Green was trying to get in touch with you yesterday but she didn't say why, only I was to tell you to telephone her urgently when you could.'

My heart leapt at the news. Betty was a local farmer's wife who lived nearby at Oak Grove Farm. I couldn't help but hope that she might have news of Toby Jug. Hurrying to

college to make my 9 a.m. lecture I was not free to telephone until much later. It was almost lunchtime before I
could break free from the tedium of student tutorials to telephone the number Helen had kindly written on the front
page of my copy of *The Times*. There was no answer although I rang several times. There was also a staff meeting
that afternoon which I had to attend and I was on edge
until it ended at 5.30 p.m. Then I was at last free to ring
Betty's number again.

The phone was answered immediately. It was Betty.

'Oh I'm so glad you rang,' she said in her soft Scottish
accent. 'It's just that I saw your notice in the Post Office
window and it started me thinking about a wee stray cat we
found in one of our byres.'

'What colour is it?' I asked with a lump in my throat, willing it to be Toby Jug. I waited, fearful of her reply.

'Well it's hard to tell 'cause it's all covered in mud but it
seems to have a black-and-white face from what we could
see. It's hard to get near it 'cause the wee thing's awful nervous. I think you'd better come over and see for yourself,' she
concluded.

I told her I'd be there as soon as I could. Filled with new
heart-thudding hope I set off at once for the farm.

Betty and Joe Green met me as I drove into the farmyard.
At the sound and sight of my car their two sheepdogs were
roused to a fit of barking, but at a soft word from Joe they

subsided to frenetic tail-wagging. It was getting dark but I saw that Betty held a huge torch the size of a lantern by her side.

'It's over in the cowshed,' Joe said, and bade the dogs to lie and stay.

It was dark and there were pungent animal smells in the shed which had a stone-tiled floor. As Betty shone her torch all I could see were lumps of mud and cow dung spattered with straw.

'It's there in the corner,' she pointed as Joe stood back lighting his pipe.

Stooping low under a wooden crossbeam I peered into the corner. Suddenly I saw him. It was Toby Jug as I'd never before seen him. Dirty and bedraggled with the pathetic look of the waif, he lay blinking his green eyes in the fierce torchlight. Relief flooded through me like a blood transfusion.

'Is it yours?' Betty's voice intruded.

'Yes!' I gasped as I picked him up and hugged him to my chest, concern for the plight he was in smarting my eyes with tears. 'Most certainly yes, he's mine all right; thank you, thank you both,' I managed to blurt out, overwhelmed as I was with relief and joy.

Betty insisted, in that kind way that farming people have, that I should come back to the farmhouse for a warm drink and some supper. I was about to put Toby Jug in the car to wait for me but Betty wouldn't hear of it.

'You must bring him into the kitchen so I can clean the wee thing up for you. I'll not be having him going back with you in that state,' she said firmly.

Joe and I sat in the farmhouse kitchen, drinking steaming mugs of hot chocolate and eating home-cooked, cinnamon-flavoured apple pie. Meanwhile, Betty washed Toby Jug in a large bathtub that she ordinarily used for the dogs. Huge but gentle hands that had delivered many a lamb and calf now cleaned and soothed my stricken Toby Jug as if he were a baby lamb. He lay still, totally compliant, with only the occasional glance in my direction, as she worked her healing charm and we ate and we talked.

It appeared that Toby Jug had been found on the day after the hunt. Joe had noticed him first. They had an enormous black cat aptly called Black Bob whom Joe saw was paying rapt attention to something in the corner of the cow byre. At first Joe thought it must be a rat then he saw that Black Bob was actually licking and attempting to groom a small cat which was caked in mud and looked half-dead. The amazing thing about it, Joe told me, was that normally Black Bob would attack and chase away any cat that invaded his territory.

'Except for that grey she-cat last Autumn,' Betty cut in. 'They ran together for days on end,' she said.

'Aye but that were different,' Joe said. 'They were mating. Black Bob's a heck of a tom cat.' He chuckled, proud of his cat's prowess. 'Come nights I could hear her wailing with the mating like, then she disappeared.'

As I listened my mind clicked with the realization that here could possibly be the final piece of the puzzle regarding the mystery of Toby Jug's parentage. It all dropped into place. I started to feel sure as I glanced at the magnificently sleek body of Black Bob lying in a rapture of warmth in front of the Aga cooker. Could it possibly be that he was Toby's father? That was why he hadn't attacked Toby Jug for invading his territory. Somehow, by means only known to cats, he had recognized his own offspring. Either that or he'd taken pity on Toby Jug, small and frightened as he would have been.

Whilst I was lost in my own thoughts, Joe had continued his account of how Toby Jug had been found. In answer to my questioning it appeared that Joe and Betty had at various times tried to catch Toby Jug and find out what was wrong with him. But since they were both quite stout in build and Toby was scared stiff, they hadn't succeeded. Joe reckoned that somehow Toby Jug had got in the way of the hunt and had fled to the farmyard. On the way he would have had to run through the mud pool at the end of the field leading to the farm. That must have been how he ended up caked in mud.

'Clarts,' Joe said, referring to the mud. 'He was covered in clarts when I first set eyes on him but what I can't understand is how Black Bob has taken to him. It's beyond me,' he finished, puffing away at his pipe.

Just as I had done with Mrs Erskins I explained what I knew to Betty and Joe.

'I knew there were something special about that silver she-cat,' Joe said. 'I could have sworn she wasn't from hereabouts.'

By this time we were all tired and Toby Jug was dry and snug, lying fast asleep next to Black Bob. It was long past midnight when Toby Jug and I left Joe and Betty at Oak Grove Farm. It had been an historic occasion in more ways than one. Toby Jug now looked little the worse for his ordeal but I knew the emotional scars would remain with him for some time. Never again would he run with the fox and hounds. I could bank on that.

In the days that followed Toby Jug gradually regained his strength and lively personality. How many lives have you left? I asked him. But he was away up the apple tree foraging for insects and the like and seemed oblivious to the threat of dangers which had now passed into his subconscious. It was great to have him back and I slept only moderately that first night of his return, waking periodically to check and reassure myself that he was asleep at the foot of my bed and that I wasn't dreaming. He had returned and was alive and well. I slept with the hope that his adventures were over for the present, at least. And I felt satisfied in my own mind that I

Just for fun, I built a snowman and a snowcat for Toby Jug.

Toby Jug went for a prowl in the snow, making paw tracks in the moonlight.

It was the anniversary of his rescue, and we both took a celebratory stroll in the snow.

I buried him under the apple tree he loved to climb, and made a solemn promise.

had finally found the cat which had fathered him. So much for the meaning of that thing called coincidence.

Soon preparations for Christmas were in full swing. There were concerts to celebrate the end of term at the college, and in Alnwick town the various churches were rehearsing for their carol services and Christmas concerts. The shops everywhere were putting up their decorations and lights. Atop the Bondgate Tower, the Duke had given permission for the town council to erect, for the first time, a neon-lit Santa Claus with sledge and reindeer. All together, the town was looking very jolly, in stark contrast to the weather which was fiercely cold and damp.

There is a special feeling about Christmas time which, for me at least, neither age nor blatant commercialism can demean. It evokes in most of us feelings of nostalgia which are vintage childhood and images of the story of the birth of Jesus, the exciting tales of Santa Claus and the opening of longed-for presents are carried with us for a lifetime. Parties and seasonal food, such as roast turkey and Christmas pudding, tend to make us as adults regress to the happy times of childhood as we waited in eager anticipation for Christmas Eve. I tried to capture this innocent spirit of Christmas in the cottage.

It would have to be an extra special celebration this year because it was Toby Jug's first Christmas and soon he would be one year old. The intense feelings that people have about Christmas can be infectious and so it proved in the cottage with Toby Jug. He joined in wholeheartedly with my own excitement when one dreary wet Sunday afternoon I began to dress the Christmas tree. The colourful baubles and strings of tinsel were a delight to him and I had to frequently restrain him from trying to leap up among the tree decorations. I have to admit that Toby's enthusiasm for life in general made the preparations for Christmas that year less of a chore and more of a shared joy. He was a great companion. With him around there was never a dull moment.

I have a tradition at Christmas which derives from my childhood days when my family lived near Axwell Park, close to Blaydon-on-Tyne. On Christmas mornings, after church and when the presents had been opened, my sisters and I would go for a walk down to the lake in the park and feed the swans. If it was a cold winter's day then we would have to break the ice at the lakeside to feed them. When the birds saw us with our pieces of bread they would leave the open water near the island where they nested and come gracefully flapping and sliding across the ice to us. It was a rare experience to be so close to these wild birds who would sometimes leave the water to be hand-fed. Images recalled from those times always come into my mind as Christmas approaches – standing in the frosted grass, under a grey sky, with the gaunt shapes of the mist-shrouded trees in the background and the coldness piercing our muffled forms, freezing our hands and ears. And then returning home to look again at our presents and feast on roast turkey with all the trimmings. These for me are among the best residues of my childhood past.

Now, at Christmas time, whenever I can I go for an early morning walk by a lake and take bread to feed the ducks and swans as a gesture to fond memories and to make a contribution to nature in the spirit of charity to all creatures. Since coming to live at the cottage I had been able to indulge this ritual by going down to the local lake just beyond St Michael's Church. This year I had a lot to be thankful for, especially because of the cat in my life, and I wanted it to be a particularly good day, one to remember.

On Christmas morning I was up and out of bed very early. Toby Jug was up before me although he often slept late on the dark mornings of winter. On this occasion he was rooting around the cottage to find one of his red balls for a solo play session. Usually, once it was daylight, I would find him staring through the bedroom window at the feathered activity on the garden bird-table. I had no central heating in the cottage then, so in winter the window panes often frosted over during the night with characteristic white starry shapes. Toby Jug, cute little beast that he was, had got into the habit of licking the window pane, probably for the sharp cold taste on his tongue but possibly so that he could see outside.

On this morning it was still dark outside and although the windowpanes were heavily frosted over he hadn't bothered with them. As I was putting on my dressing gown he joined me and we went downstairs together. I laboured to clear and light the fire as he kept nudging my legs with his head to remind me that he wanted his breakfast. Normally, I fed him first before I did anything else. Today was different, but he had no way of knowing that. I didn't want to feed him just at that moment because we would be having roast turkey for lunch so he had to suffice with a saucer of milk and a small portion of dried cat food. This did not go down at all well with him and he kept following me about and darting between my legs. Several times I almost tripped over him.

Having started the fire and sipped a few mouthfuls of hot tea, I got the car out at once, whilst it was still dark, because there was much to do. Since we could not go to the nearby lake in the woods as there were no longer any ducks there, Toby Jug and I set off for Bolam Lake which was several miles away.

Driving beneath a black and sullen sky we drove towards the lake deep in the Rothbury Hills. I like driving on country roads when there is nobody else about and on this morning our car was the first to make tracks on the white, frost-covered road. Toby Jug sat on the back of the front passenger seat staring fixedly ahead, excited at where we were going at this unusual time in the morning. As we rounded a particularly sharp bend a barn owl flapped away in front of us, carrying something in its talons, probably a rat. Toby Jug almost fell off his perch trying to see more of this ghostly white marauder. It was sights like this, of nature in the raw, that made me happy to be living in these parts.

As we drew near to the lake the sky, although clouded, began to brighten ever so slightly. I parked the car between two thick oak trees close to the water. The first orange glow of dawn silhouetted the dark shapes of willows against the frosted lakeside. The lake itself remained hidden beneath long wisps of smoky mist lying just above the surface. I collected a bag of scraps from the car boot and strolled towards the water's edge, my boots crunching in the frozen carpet of leaves. Toby Jug was scampering along eagerly at my heels and glancing up at me now and again, his green eyes reflecting the early dawn light. He loved having new experiences as much as I did and he wasn't the least bit afraid as long as we were together. He trotted with his nose held high to sniff the air and to fully relish the scents and sights of this new place.

As I had hoped, the swans and the ducks were there, emerging eerily through the mist to consume the scraps of food I tossed them. Some of the ducks waded ashore, jostling each other for the morsels I'd dropped. Toby Jug and the ducks eyed each other suspiciously and he retreated to my side in the face of their advance. As for the ducks, hunger won the day over any apprehensions they might have had about cats. Toby wasn't the sort of cat to attack a full-grown duck but I expect the ducks couldn't be sure about that. The swans didn't even leave the water, stretching their elegant necks instead to take the best morsels for themselves. At the sight of them, floating serenely nearer to us, Toby Jug leapt on to my shoulder and gazed at them with awe. He'd never seen birds as big as this before and they were making quite a strong impression on him.

Shaking the last crumbs from the bag I suddenly felt a shiver run through me and when I looked I could see that Toby's fur was fully fluffed out in reaction to the cold. The quiet stillness of the dawn we had briefly witnessed was being swept away by a chill wind making wavelets on the lake and ruffling the feathers of the ducks. As the mist dispersed I could see the swans swimming away to the sheltered side of the lake in the lee of some pine trees. It was time to wish them and the ducks a 'Merry Christmas and a Happy New Year', and to go home. We hurried back to the comfort of the car, our good deed done and family tradition intact.

By the time we arrived back home it was full daylight but dull and cold so that we needed all the lights on in the house. The fire, which I'd banked with coal before leaving, was a welcome red mass of heat and Toby Jug and I huddled round it to warm ourselves, me with my back to it and he staring straight into the burning coals. It was time for a festive drink. For Toby Jug it was a saucer of warm evaporated milk; for me it was a glass of hot mulled wine. I toasted his health and wished him a Happy Christmas and he reciprocated by jumping on my shoulder and licking my ear. Now it was time to open the presents that I'd placed under the Christmas tree.

Mine were an assortment of ties, socks and a shirt from my mother and sisters. Diane Forester, the colleague at work whose horse I had looked after during the summer months, had bought me a litre bottle of cognac from the French resort where she and the family had spent the summer holidays. It was especially welcome.

Toby Jug, full of curiosity as usual, playfully pounced and dived among the present wrappings and ribbons as if their sole purpose had been for his amusement. There were two presents for him. One was a deluxe cat basket which was built along the lines of an igloo. It had a fluffy, washable mat inside and outside, on the red-coloured fabric, in bold black letters it bore the name 'Toby Jug'. After thoroughly inspecting it with his nose he climbed inside and lay down as if he'd decided that this was what was expected of him.

When I came to open his second present he was still inside, so I had to lift him out to present him with a brand new red leather fur-lined cat collar complete with three bells and a new address disc. I'd added the bells to his collar because recently I'd seen him suspiciously eyeballing some of the songbirds, especially a robin redbreast, in the cottage garden. It would also keep me aware of his movements and stop me worrying when we went walking together and he wandered off to the side and flanked me through the woods.

The presents were a great success but the highlight of the day for Toby Jug was the Christmas lunch. He disgraced himself by demanding so many helpings of turkey, followed by a sizeable dish of fresh cream, that afterwards he could only just make it as far as the sitting room. He was quite incapable, as well as unwilling, to move from his place by the fire for the rest of the day. He surreptitiously opened only one eye as I left the cottage for an evening visit to church, but remained lying there stretched out in absolute contentment, the epitome of a relaxed cat. As I left the room, teasing him about his overfed state (to which he literally didn't even blink an eye), an age-old saying came to mind, 'A greedy man's wagon is never full'.

Toby Jug's first Christmas and New Year were truly memorable for all sorts of reasons but especially for the friendliness and joy he brought into my life. I had never known a cat like him. On the one hand he was as extroverted and friendly as a little dog but on the other hand he professed the independence and introverted self-containment of the proverbial cat. The unique way in which he had been reared by me had a lot to do with his personality, I'm sure, but there was also his Maine Coon inheritance. This was also an influential factor. Every living thing has singular qualities which make it different from others, even creatures of the same species and breed. Toby Jug, because of the conditions of his early environment, was most definitely a one-off.

As well the domestic life he had with me in the cottage and which he appeared to enjoy to the full, Toby Jug responded to the primitive call of the wild. Increasingly, he displayed the innermost urge to wander at will in the fields and woods near our home for longer periods of time. He was assuredly my pet cat but he was also his own cat. I had worried at times that because I had been so instrumental in his upbringing he might become something of a neurotic house cat, afraid of his own natural instincts and terrified to leave the safety of the cottage. I was very relieved to observe that, while his close attachment to me was indisputable, Toby Jug had enough of a wild streak to give him his natural rights and dignity as an animal.

In this respect I didn't scold him when just after New Year he brought me a present of a mouse which he'd killed and, some days later, a weasel; I praised him for the clever cat he was. To my knowledge he never did kill a bird. I believe that he knew that somehow I wouldn't be happy with him if he did that. I had told him so and perhaps he understood me and respected my wishes but I sensed he didn't like birds at all, especially big birds. His hunt adventure and near death in the jaws of the foxhounds had taught him to be cannier in his wanderings. For all that, though, Toby Jug had a life and a mind of his own.

Sometimes when I was returning home whilst it was still daylight, I would stop the car on a hill, in a parking bay by the roadside, overlooking the countryside adjacent to the cottage. Then I would take out the binoculars I carried with me in the car and scan the fields and hedgerows for Toby Jug. He was quite distinctive with his white vest and white paws and I could literally see him a mile away.

On one particular occasion I spotted him investigating every ditch and tree stump along his way, happily unaware of the fact that I was watching his every move. I was proud to see him doing his own thing. Another time, in late October, I caught sight of him stalking rabbits in the stubble of a hayfield. All at once he stopped sniffing the grass in front of him and looked directly at me, his face so intent in my eyeglasses that it startled me. It was as if he could see me. But then I rationalized it by telling myself that it was probably something in the foreground which had caught his eye.

However, there are stories about cats that suggest they may have psychic powers and maybe, just maybe, Toby Jug sensed that I was there. Uncanny as it might seem, on the day when I thought he'd become aware of me watching him through binoculars, he was there to greet me at the gate when I drove in. What this meant was that even if he'd taken his own shortcuts, he must have covered about a mile on foot whilst I drove in a round about way four miles along the twisting road. Cats are incredible creatures and there were many times that Toby Jug impressed me with just how incredible a cat he was.

Of course, I continued to worry about him. One incident which startled me happened when I was taking my habitual evening stroll through the garden, waiting to see the bats. Toby Jug was somewhere close about when a car braked hard and screeched to a stop in the roadway fronting the cottage and then hastily roared off. Almost at once a long-haired tortoiseshell cat streaked up my drive and suddenly dropped in her tracks. I hurried over to find a lovely cat in her death throes. Obviously, she had been hit by the car I had just heard. There wasn't anything I could do for her as she was bleeding badly from the mouth and had most certainly been ruptured inside. I knelt by her and tried to comfort her by gently stroking her head and within a short time she convulsed and died.

Just after this happened there came a sound from nearby which was so eerie it made the hairs stand up on the back of my neck and sent a cold shudder right through me. It was

Toby Jug, a short distance away, staring at the dead cat and emitting a deep hollow sound which I'd never heard before nor since and which I can best describe as a cat howl. It was unearthly to hear and so blood-chilling that it filled me with fear. I went to him and gathered him up in my arms. His body was trembling. Pacifying him at length, I shut him in the cottage. I then gathered up the dead cat and laid it in a prominent place by the roadside, hoping its owner would find the body and at least know what had happened to it. The dead cat wore a collar but no address tag so I just had to leave it there.

In the morning I looked out for it but the body and the plastic bag on which I'd placed it had gone. Toby Jug was most upset that night and insisted on sleeping near me on the bed even though he'd become accustomed to sleeping in his new igloo in the bedroom. I concluded from these strange happenings that, although I know a lot about cats, there are still a lot of things that cats know that I do not.

Literature about the Maine Coon emphasises that this breed is remarkably intelligent. From my own experience with cats I can support this statement. I found Toby Jug to be extraordinarily clever, which was all the more surprising in view of his traumatic start in life. He proved to be the brightest of all the cats I have known. Not wishing to demean those other clever animals in any way, Toby Jug was superior. A great deal of what made Toby Jug so exceptional was that, although I knew him well in so many ways, there were things about him that remained a mystery to me. This is what made our relationship fascinating. I had, in him, a piece of pure and profound cat nature.

Shortly after the turn of the year the weather changed for the worst in the Coquet Valley, as so often happens in these parts of Northumberland. A significant date was looming in my mind which at one time I hadn't dared even think about, let alone hope for. It was the date of the anniversary of finding Toby Jug. On 21 January, it would be one complete year from the time when I had set out in the snow to rescue his mother and found her kittens. I determined to make it a special occasion.

As I was driving back from work, it started to snow and by the time I reached the cottage it was falling heavily enough to lay a thick white carpet on the road. The weather closed in exactly as it had done the previous year. It snowed as if it would never stop. Roads were becoming blocked, while bushes, trees, fells and hills all around became lost in the snowscape.

Toby Jug was waiting for me under the protective umbrella of the giant fir tree and came bounding to greet me as I alighted from the car. He leapt on to my shoulder and began the welcome home routine that I now knew so well and looked forward to so much (even though the left shoulder of all my jackets were beginning to have a somewhat worn look).

That evening, as a celebration, I cooked us both a tasty meal of fresh cod in a white creamy sauce. I had a glass of claret and Toby had a saucer of evaporated milk just for old time's sake. Afterwards, I built up the huge fire grate with some of the logs I'd cut in summer until there was enough heat from their blaze to chase away any of the cold memories left in my mind of that tragic night the previous year. For a while Toby Jug lay on my knees, all warm and fluffy, as he snuggled into my old sweater, which he had made a tattered remnant of its former glory. I looked him over as I stroked him. He had grown into a really fine-looking cat. He had a sturdy body and a healthy coat of silken fur. Moreover, he had a strong character and a loveable personality. Above all, Toby Jug was a real companion and I thought of him only in the dearest terms.

Casting my mind back to the beginning I considered it remarkable that one year ago tonight he had lain in an open barn, dying of starvation and hypothermia. Had it merely been chance or was it some other agent of serendipity that had lured me away from a cosy fireside to encounter a tragic drama that was to change my life for the better? When I thought deeply about it I couldn't decide who had been really rescued, Toby Jug or me. From a philosophical viewpoint I reckon it was mutual.

Later that evening I went to the back door from where I'd heard Toby Jug's mother screaming in pain on that night which seemed such a long time ago. There was no screaming this night, only deep powdery snowdrifts all around. For the moment the air was clear and the stars were out with a bright half-moon dominating the sky. The countryside was like an enchanting new country. Although I knew it well, that night it seemed wonderfully unfamiliar. The stars were brilliant against the black blanket of the sky, their light appearing to reflect on the snow and ice.

Toby Jug came to the door to see what I was doing. He looked out and decided to go for a prowl. At first he wasn't sure about this deep white stuff but I saw that he was analysing this experience of snow as yet another of nature's challenges. Possibly it was something that could be turned into a plaything like leaves blowing in the wind or the wavering tall grasses that were fun to charge. It was as if he couldn't quite work out why he kept slipping through the powdery surfaces. I chuckled at the sight of the puzzled expression on his face as he tried to work out how a seemingly solid surface could suddenly give way. He didn't like to see me laughing at him and he whined with the frustration of it all. As he became accustomed to the snow he romped through it with abandon. I watched him overcome his caution at this new experience and he scooted exuberantly here and there. Even though I was growing cold and starting to shiver I stayed to watch his antics, unable to tear myself away from the sight of him enjoying himself.

Then I vividly recalled his mother and the paw tracks of her desperate flight in the moonlight to rejoin her kittens – paw tracks in the snow which I had followed and which led me to the sick kitten that was now a healthy, full-grown cat. Moving to my warm refuge in the sitting room, I watched him through the window making his own paw tracks in the moonlight. No parent could have been prouder. It was a singularly happy ending to the year for both of us.

Soon, Toby was once again lying by the fire.

'Well,' I said, 'if it stays fair tomorrow we'll have some more fun in the snow.'

Toby looked doubtful, wondering how I could think of something as silly as that. Then we both settled down to an evening of reflection, gently toasting ourselves by the blazing log fire. I sipped a glass of brandy. Toby curled himself into a ball and purred loudly. I wondered if he remembered what happened a year ago. I certainly did.

When morning came, the sky was blue and it didn't look as if it would snow again. The freezing air made the snow crisp underfoot and, as Toby and I scrunched our way across the garden, on impulse and for the boyish pleasure of it, I decided to build a snowman. Later, I was joined by an inquisitive Toby Jug who watched me at work from what he considered a safe distance. To please him further, I made a snowcat for him.

SAYING GOODBYE

Toby Jug lived with me for a further eleven years, during which time we shared a lot of life together and I was impressed time and again by his remarkable character and personality. He was by nature an extremely loving cat with an attractively affable attitude to life. We continued to have many wonderful adventures together after this traumatic, eventful, but wonderful first year.

The manner of his dying is for me an especially sad topic to write about. I think we all tend to imagine the future in terms of our awareness of the present, with all its assurances and comforts – we expect the good times to last forever. Toby Jug matured over the years into a fine cat but within a short time his life was ended with a suddenness that was impossible to understand. Not for him the gentle descent into old age and the eventual death in his sleep after a full and happy life. He was stricken with an agonizing spell of acute suffering in which I was powerless to help him. I would have done anything imaginable to save his life but it was not to be. He died just two days after his twelfth birthday, having been ill for several weeks. I'm afraid that veterinary science was not as well developed in the 1970s as it is now and there was nothing that could be done for his condition.

It happened like this. One day he whined in pain as he ate his food and seemed sickly all evening. I examined him as carefully as I could and scrutinized his mouth and teeth thoroughly. I could find nothing of significance. The following day he did his rounds of the garden as usual in the morning but he seemed to want only to lie around on the floor panting all day. During my lunch break I came home to check him out. There didn't seem to be any improvement but nor did he appear to be really ill either. Just a shade off-colour, as my grandmother would have said.

When I fed him that evening he was able to eat his food but something was wrong. He whined all the while he was chewing. I decided he must have an abscess or something else wrong with his teeth. Mac's veterinary surgery had by now been sold off and his surgery demolished to make way for a block of flats so I had to search in the phone book for a suitable vet.

Eventually, I found an address and carried Toby Jug in my arms into the car where he lay on my lap as I drove to this new veterinary surgery in the village of Stobswood. It was so unlike him just to lie and snuggle into my lap in the car that I began to feel more than worried: I began to feel afraid. There was a crowd in the surgery, some of the people had small animals, but there were no other cats. There were, however, some noisy dogs who seemed prone to bark incessantly. Toby Jug clung desperately to me throughout the ordeal of waiting and at long last we were ushered into the consulting room.

Gently, I laid him on the table in the room and stood back as the vet began to examine him. It seemed to take ages but throughout it all Toby Jug never once whimpered or demurred at the intimacies of the examination. At last the vet addressed me.

'I can't find anything wrong with his teeth or mouth. His stomach and insides did not cause any distress when I prodded him. He possibly has some kind of infection which is causing him gastric upset and I suggest that you put him on a milky pudding-type diet for a few days and see if there is any improvement. Give him a few days more and if there is no change in his condition then bring him back to see me. He is a small cat, isn't he?'

I could not for the life of me understand this latter remark and found it rather insulting.

Toby Jug got worse. A few days after the visit to the vet he wouldn't eat at all and he became incontinent. I took him back to the vet and was given tablets which he wouldn't take. He took to lying in his box all day, seemingly unable to stir abroad, and I tended him as I had done when he was a kitten. I tried to feed him on the baby mixture that I had given him so many years before but all to no avail. He constantly cried out with the agony of whatever it was afflicting him and I found it unbearable to hear him suffering. Once more we made our way to the vet.

Whilst being examined in the surgery he vomited and whined painfully. I winced at the sounds of his pain, all the more so because I couldn't do a thing to ease him. The duty vet that particular morning, a young woman, was very gentle with him and I could tell she liked cats because she stroked and spoke to Toby as she examined him. She called for the veterinary nurse and asked for a particular instrument which, when it came, I thought I recognized an ophthalmoscope. With this instrument she carefully examined Toby Jug's eyes and then took a blood sample from him which she analysed with the help of a modern-looking machine.

When she finished her examination she looked sadly at me and my heart fell.

'I'm so sorry,' she said as she slowly stroked Toby's back. 'I realize how much you love your cat but I'm afraid he has a brain tumour and there is nothing I can do for him except put him out of his misery.'

I felt dead inside as her words sunk in. I looked at Toby Jug and he looked at me. He knew he was dying, I could tell it in his eyes. The vet moved away from the table and opened the door to leave.

'I'll give you a few minutes privacy to say your goodbyes,'

she said. 'You'll be doing the best thing you can for him in the circumstances and he will not feel any pain, I assure you.'

And with that she closed the door and we were alone, just Toby Jug and me.

'I'm sorry, Toby Jug. There's nothing more I can do for you, pal,' I said lamely. 'I wish I could ask you what you want me to do about this.'

I whispered more to myself than to him. With the full re-alization of what was about to happen the tears began unashamedly running down my cheeks. With a heartfelt sigh and wiping my eyes with the sleeve of my jacket, I made my decision and was about to recall the vet to tell her to take Toby Jug away. Suddenly, Toby moved from the prone position in which the vet had left him and, in spite of his condition, began slowly and painfully to move towards where I was standing at the side of the table. To my aston-ishment he began to climb with great difficulty up my jacket until his front paws reached my left shoulder and there he clung with desperation, despite his weakness. I put my arm around him for support and cried at the message he'd given me. Toby Jug had given me his answer. He wanted to go home to die.

This situation mirrored the time almost twelve years ago when I first took a very ill kitten back to my home to live. Now I was taking Toby Jug to our home to die. The door opened and the vet came in expecting me to leave Toby Jug with her. She was surprised to see him clinging on to my shoulder. I explained how I felt and what I understood Toby Jug to be feeling. She took our decision very well and even offered to give me two prepared syringes containing a powerful painkiller which she advised me to use when it became necessary. Finally, she gave me her prognosis which was that Toby Jug would probably die within the next forty-eight hours.

'Keep him warm and comfortable and let nature do the rest,' she advised as I was leaving with Toby Jug and a packet containing the two syringes.

When I arrived back at the cottage I lifted him out of the car and he seemed to brighten at the familiar sights and scents, but I could tell that he was very poorly. I considered somehow killing him myself for his sake, to put him out of his misery, but then hastily rejected the notion. I didn't know how and if I had known I could never have brought myself to do it. Nor could I bring myself to take him back to the vet to be put down, to be put to sleep as it is euphemistically called. Not my Toby Jug. We had faced lots of crises together and now we would just have to do our best to see this one though to the end.

As it turned out I didn't need to use the pain killer injections because he no longer cried out with pain. Perhaps his brain's endorphins had taken over and were relieving him of suffering in these final moments of his life. I certainly hoped so. Two-and-a-half weeks after my initial visit to the vet, Toby Jug died.

It was a day after our last visit that it happened, well within the vet's prognosis. The night before his death I had placed him in a newly lined box to make him as comfortable as possible and, having washed and cleaned him for the umpteenth time, I suddenly felt so drained of energy and worn out with distress that I was almost in a state of collapse. I had to sleep but I couldn't leave him alone and it was impractical to take him to bed with me. Instead, I moved his box near to the settee in the living room where we had shared so much living. Stoking the fire to keep out the wintry cold, I lit the candles for both our sakes.

Although I was very tired I took time to talk to him as I bade him goodnight. As I stroked and softly spoke to him, I told him how much I loved him and how wonderful he was. At my words he reared up from his lying position and pushed his forehead and face into my hand and gave me a throaty purr, just the once. I felt so much affection for him that I found it almost impossible to consider that he would ever die. Toby Jug was the super cat who could survive anything. I had believed we would enjoy life together for many more years.

Pulling my winter overcoat over me I lay back on the settee and, with only the flickering light from the coal fire and the candles to illuminate the room, I whispered goodnight to Toby Jug once more. I then fell into the deepest of all sleeps that only exhaustion can bring. It was the last time I saw him alive.

The next morning I found him dead in his box. Rigor mortis had set in, so he must have died shortly after I went to sleep. Even though part of me knew he was dying, the reality of his death shocked me more than anything I had ever experienced. I was totally devastated. I had lost something that I could never regain and which had been such a living treasure to me.

I considered what I had to do as I mechanically sipped my morning brew of tea. He wasn't there anymore for me but I had to be there for him. I shaved and dressed for work. Recently, I had been appointed to a lectureship at Newcastle University and I had twenty-nine students waiting for me to tutor them that morning. I didn't know how I was going to do it but there was no one else to take my place. The mourning for Toby Jug would have to go on mental hold. However, his burial would not wait. I couldn't face the prospect of coming home to the sight of his dead body.

I rushed upstairs and selected my very best sweater, a blue lamb's-wool one that I had bought myself last Christmas. For purely sentimental reasons, I couldn't bring myself to give up the tattered ones which he liked so well. Slipping on the pair of Wellingtons I used for gardening, I carried his body outside. In the misty early morning I dug a hole at least four feet deep in the frosted ground under the gnarled old apple tree that he loved to climb. I held his cold stiff body for a long moment, the last time I would ever see him, and consoled myself with the thought that wherever he was he wasn't here any more. Wrapping him hastily in the sweater, I buried him along with a few of his remaining red balls, his food trays and a cushion on which he liked to lie. I placed his body on the cushion at the bottom of the grave.

After I filled in his grave I made him a solemn promise. Flushed with emotion and through my tears, I promised him that I would some day write and publish the story of his life. I wanted to share with the rest of the world the special memories that I had of him and our life together. I felt that I had to preserve the uniqueness of our experience if only to relieve my own pain and sadness at his loss. He was gone from me now but I would never forget him.

This I promised him in all good faith but I never imagined at the time how difficult it would be to keep that promise. I had kept diary notes and taken photographs but the latter were unfortunately lost when I moved houses. Still, I have an excellent memory that has served me in good stead as a teacher and lecturer. Over the years I made several attempts at writing the story of our life together but none of them worked. Then, when I took early retirement from full-time work, I decided to have a final go, prompted by my wife Catherine who had long suffered my stories about Toby Jug.

This book is testament to the fulfilment of my promise and to the enduring love of cats that was Toby Jug's legacy to me.

Five months after his death I sold the cottage because I found that I couldn't go on living there with the heartache of his loss. I moved far away so that I could begin a new life. Friends advised me to get another kitten and some were offered but I couldn't at that time bring myself to take on a new pet. Because of the way I felt, it wouldn't have been fair to either the kitten or to me. At that time I did not think that I would see Owl Cottage ever again, only fate has a way of making the unexpected happen – but that's another story.

Some four years after Toby's death, I was engaged for a short time as a psychological consultant for a Tyne Tees Television programme called *Friday Live*. On a wintry night in January, after one of the shows about the topic of 'Psychic Phenomena and Clairvoyance', the celebrity cast and I were enjoying the TV company's hospitality at a local hotel. One of the psychic experts, who had been demonstrating her skills on this particular programme, stopped by my chair as I was sitting chatting with some of the cast.

Placing a hand on my shoulder to attract my attention she leaned close to my head and, speaking in a hushed voice so that only I could hear, she gave me an astounding message. What she said brought tears to my eyes and yet, oddly enough, always gives me comfort whenever I think of it, even if I find it hard to believe.

She said: 'I am tired out with my efforts this evening but I just had to tell you what I've seen because it might be an important message for you. When you walked over to the bar just now I was aware of a spirit animal following you. Did you once have a black-and-white cat that you cared for very much? The initials T and J come to mind. Does that have any meaning for you?'

Choking back long-forgotten emotions, I was quite unable to speak. I simply nodded.

'Well,' she said, smiling at the look on my face, 'he's sitting on your shoulder right now!'